THE SOUTHERN WAY

Issue No 24

CONTENTS

© Kevin Robertson (Noodle Books) and the various contributors 2013

ISBN 978-1-909328-09-9

First published in 2013 by Kevin Robertson

under the **NOODLE BOOKS** imprint

PO Box 279

Corhampton

SOUTHAMPTON

SO32 3ZX

www.noodlebooks.co.uk

editorial@thesouthernway.co.uk

Printed in England by

Berforts Information Press Ltd.

Editorial

I think sometimes we can all become blinkered in our views and interests, whether that be relative to railways or whatever. I will not divulge my own specific railway preferences although I will admit I have been deliberately very careful with 'SW' both in this and preceding issues to ensure a particular personal favourite does not dominate the pages. (In fact I can safely say my own choice has rarely appeared in print!) Why do I mention this? Well it occurred to me whilst browsing the internet the other evening that I was looking at the same few sites time and time again. Little had changed on what was a daily basis, but a little sideways diversion and a whole new vista of interest appears.

What has this to do with railways and 'SW'? Simply this, our lead article. Now let me say at the outset, I have often felt that any book that needs a note on the actual cover 'Introduction by *a well known person*' is almost an excuse to say the content is possibly a bit thin and the book therefore needs a prop at the start. Of course those in marketing will strongly disagree and there may well be justification in certain cases. So to return to 'SW', I mention this because the lead article for this issue is on Mr Maunsell and describes how much his previous life in Ireland influenced his work on the SECR and in turn the SR.

We as a nation of enthusiasts are often 'conservative' in our attitudes. I know what I like, (I may know a limited amount about other railways) but individually we are probably unlikely to dig deeply into areas away from our preference. If the opposite were the case, then publishers would probably sell an identical number of copies of every book they produced. I can promise that is certainly not the case. I will also admit I am ever grateful to the regular band of followers who either subscribe or purchase 'SW' every time, and who trust the content will relate to their favourite railway, I could not manage without you. but these individuals will have the complete issue in front of them ready to read or dip into as they wish. What worries me slightly is that by digressing very slightly on to a subject which in this case shows why Mr Maunsell acted the way he did on the SR, the very subject 'Maunsell before the SECR/SR' might be seen as of lesser interest. Having obviously read the piece before it appeared in print I can assure you that is not the case. Am I then giving this article a prop? I hope not, that is certainly not what is intended and anyway it does not need it. The very fact it appears as the lead article should in itself indicate the importance placed upon the content. Author Jeremy Clements is a man who does take a wider view, he too no doubt has his preferences, but he should also be complimented for compiling what is a fascinating and original piece of research and well up to the standard of work in his separate books on the GSR and William Dean.

We move on to sadder news. As I was in the process of preparing this issue I was informed of the sad passing of Tony Goodyear. Tony was a retired signal engineer from the Southern Region, also a man with a considerable grasp of history. His contributions to 'SW' were there almost from the start, sometimes in the form of a word or useful piece of advice, and more recently as compiler of the series 'The Southern Railway from Inception to Nationalisation', Part 5 of which appeared in 'SW23'. It was a privilege to be invited to attend the service of thanksgiving. He will be sadly missed and I know you will join me in extending condolences to his family and Pauline in particular.

Finally, it does not take a mathematician to work out that in January we reach a milestone, Issue No 25 of 'the Southern Way'. As I prepare this in July / August I can already say Mike King will feature in the lead article with Part 1 of 'Southern Utility Vans'. There will also be more from Peter Tatlow and Jeff Grayer As regards the rest - just wait and see! As ever, thank you for your support.

Kevin Robertson

Front cover - *Within the dark interior of Eastleigh shed, USA No 30064 awaits its next duty: the 'Not to be Moved' board will be noted. Derek Fear*

Pages 2/3 - *A view with a difference. Diesel-electric No 10201 needs no introduction (remember Nos 10201/2 differed in detail from No 10203, indeed the three engines formed the subject of our first 'Special Issue' on the 'Southern Main Line Diesels' but now out of print. A few new views have appeared since but nothing like this, granted it is away from the Southern during the second phase of the locomotives' lives on the LMR, but we have never seen anything with the corridor connection fitted. Was the equipment hidden behind the door or as appears more likely, fitted when required? If the latter, what was it doing attached to No 10201 and does this mean the two engines operated in multiple on the LMR in the same way we know the LMS twins Nos 10001/10002 did? It just goes to prove that no matter how much is unearthed, someone will come up with more. (Many thanks to Jeremy Clements for locating the view.)*

Opposite - *Lymington Town down starting signal and fixed distant for Lymington Pier. There was only a short half-mile section between the two stations. The low height of the post was determined by the need to afford visibility to the driver as he approached the train shed. In the background can be seen the connection to the cattle-pens, landing stage and the private Lant's siding - the gate for which is just visible across the track. (A photographic feature on Lymington Town appears on pages 36 to 41. Peter Elliott*

Rear cover - *Having referred to the 'Z' class in the lead article we thought it only fitting that one of these magnificent machines should feature in colour. No 30952 is depicted at Eastleigh. Ron Roberts.*

Above - *Great Southern & Western Railway 4-4-0 Class 52 was typical of the size and style of locomotives used in the late 19th Century, prior to the changes of the Coey/ Maunsell era. This class was introduced in 1883 by Aspinall as an enlargement of McDonnell's famous "Kerry Bogies". The class eventually totalled twenty, No 1 was one of the last built in March 1890 and was withdrawn in 1955. Five different types of boiler were fitted to this class and No 1 is carrying the raised round-topped saturated version, retaining the traditional GS&WR double (and rather leaky) smoke box doors. This was the third and last boiler type to be carried, being fitted sometime between 1935 and 1940. GS&WR tenders were another complex subject; that depicted carried 4 tons of coal and 1864 gallons of water and was one of 116 built at Inchicore and by SharpeStewart and Beyer Peacock between 1867 and 1890. It has been "modernised" by addition of side fenders but some lasted in original condition until almost the end of steam on CIE. Sister No 59 was the best-known of all Irish locomotives being the star of The Quiet Man, a 1952 Republic Production that also featured John Wayne, Maureen O' Hara and Barry Fitzgerald.*

(GREAT) SOUTHERN WAY: MAUNSELL'S PARALLEL UNIVERSE

Jeremy Clements

Until the early 1920s, Irish locomotive engineering was effectively an extension of the British industry, and the integrated nature of this relationship is apparent through certain distinguished names that appeared both sides of the water – McDonnell, Attock/ Atock, Aspinall, Ivatt, Robinson, Morton and not least, Richard Maunsell.

His later career with the South Eastern & Chatham and Southern railways is extensively documented, but Maunsell's work prior to moving to Ashford in 1913 is not so well known. This is a pity as the rich texture of his earlier experiences was to prove valuable to the SECR/ Southern. Further, these attributes enabled him comfortably to occupy the dual roles of CME with one railway company while acting as *de facto* senior consulting engineer to another. Richard Maunsell is often viewed in the context of the comparatively few steam locomotives introduced under his auspices, but consideration of the broader scope of his work, and of his international influence suggests that he was the most underrated of Britain's senior locomotive engineers in the 20th Century.

Early in his career he demonstrated an independence of spirit and a commitment to hard work by achieving an MA at Trinity College, Dublin while concurrently serving from 1888 as a pupil to HA Ivatt at the Inchicore works of the Great Southern & Western Railway. His solicitor father had been anxious for Maunsell to take up a career in the law and hoped that a degree from Trinity would extinguish his obsession with engineering. That Richard was successful in this contest of wills was evident in his transfer after three years to the Lancashire & Yorkshire Railway at Horwich, under an arrangement between Ivatt and Aspinall to exchange promising young men to broaden their experience. (Colleagues at Horwich included Hoy, Hughes and Fowler, all of whom became chief mechanical engineers, demonstrating how the seeds were sewn of the CME's "club").

In early 1892, Maunsell was appointed Locomotive Foreman in charge of three sheds in the Blackpool district, a demanding position, especially in the summer months. (Seen as a good training post, Gresley was given this job in 1900). After two years and with Aspinall's blessing, he became Assistant Divisional Locomotive Superintendent with the East India Railway. His spell in India brought rapid promotion, his final position being District Locomotive Superintendent at Asansol near Calcutta. Nevertheless, for personal reasons he wished to return to Europe and had ensured that through his father's Dublin contacts, he remained well informed of developments on the GS&WR. In 1896 HA Ivatt succeeded the recently deceased Patrick Stirling at the (English) Great Northern Railway and was replaced at Inchicore by Robert Coey. Negotiations followed by cable with Maunsell in India, leading to his appointment as Assistant Locomotive Engineer and Works Manager i.e. as Coey's deputy.

Maunsell was by then recognised as an able leader with a relaxed manner. These qualities, combined with his technical ability, contributed to the respect he enjoyed at Inchicore and to the warm relations he maintained there for the rest of his career. At the age of 28 years, he had changed employer three times, gaining broad practical experience in the process. Each move was avowedly for self-advancement, yet he stayed on friendly terms with all concerned during this peripatetic period.

Inchicore: 1896 to 1913

Return home occurred during a significant period. The GS&WR was enjoying substantial traffic growth and Inchicore under Coey was building a record for engineering excellence. Motive power until then had comprised mainly 2-4-0, 4-4-0 & 0-6-0 tender engines plus 0-4-4T, 2-4-2T & 4-4-2T types. They were well constructed but on the small side and of delightfully archaic appearance.

Modernisation commenced in 1900 with the first of 34 passenger 4-4-0s divided into five classes. They were of

Opposite bottom - *Totalling eight locomotives built 1907/8, Class 333 with 5' 8" driving wheels was Coey's last 4-4-0 type and intended for the hilly and severely curved Cork to Rosslare route. Three earlier 4-4-0 classes with 6' 7" driving wheels bore a strong family resemblance. Development of the tapered boiler was specifically Maunsell's responsibility and a total of the twenty-six 4-4-0s dating from before 1913 carried this feature at some stage in their careers. They were the only tapered boilers built at Inchicore before it was concluded that the extra construction cost was not justified. No 340 was the final class member and one of four fitted with the unusual outside frame bogie to relieve overheating of the axle journals, and to improve riding. These measures soon proved unnecessary as better lubrication solved these problems. Nevertheless, this curious arrangement was repeated when the GSR introduced five new examples of the type in 1936*

Although recorded as a Coey/ Maunsell joint design, in reality No 341 Sir William Goulding was the very first Maunsell 4-4-0 introduced in 1913. Apart from small tank engines, the naming of a GS&WR tender engine was unusual and in this case honoured the Chairman of the GS&WR Board who went on to lead the Great Southern Railways but passed away in 1925. Piston valves, superheating, Belpaire firebox and Walschaerts valve gear placed this engine firmly in the modern era. It was a potent performer, popular with crews and very much better than Watson's prototype 4-cylinder 4-6-0 No 400 that appeared in 1916. Watson had no interest in expanding Class 341 despite it being rumoured that frames had been cut for three more. No 341's later career was rather sad as despite its competence, it became something of an orphan and was withdrawn in 1928, to widespread criticism among locomotive crews and the enthusiast community. An important aspect of No 341 was weight. It was confined to the Dublin-Cork route and at the insistence of the civil engineer was weighed every six months to confirm that his restrictions had not been transgressed. Maunsell obviously learned an important lesson that bore fruit later in rebuilding SECR 4-4-0s.   *Real Photographs Co Ltd*

traditional design but introduced certain innovative features. All had round-topped fireboxes but several were fitted with tapered boilers between 1904 and 1913, the only boilers of this style constructed at Inchicore (the Class 800 4-6-0s of 1939-1940 had parallel boilers beneath tapered cladding). Another significant step was the fitting of a Schmidt superheater to one of the 4-4-0s in 1912.

The later story of the GS&WR 4-4-0s was complex with bewildering re-buildings and re-classifications but these early modifications highlighted a commitment to explore fresh initiatives. Tapered boilers were a hallmark of the Dean/ Churchward transition on the GWR and the GS&WR's adoption of this feature was one of the first applications of this concept elsewhere. Likewise, the installation of a superheater was a comparatively early response to another GWR-led initiative.

Another influence was at work following the last major expansion of the GS&WR through the takeover of the Waterford Limerick & Western Railway in 1901. The WLWR had only 33 locomotives but they looked more modern than their Inchicore contemporaries and displayed a particular elegance, especially the largest which was a trio of 4-4-0s. Maunsell's position at Inchicore was obviously secure as no employment offer was made to the WLWR's Locomotive Superintendent who had designed this fleet. In any event he had already been appraised of an opportunity with the Great Central Railway; his name was JG Robinson.

Coey retired with poor health in 1911 and was

succeeded by Maunsell. At this time the final GS&WR 4 -4-0, No 341 *Sir William Goulding*, was being planned. Although traditionally attributed as a Coey/ Maunsell design, this engine's novel features and the background circumstances suggest that it was the work of the younger man. Its parallel boiler was substantially larger than those of the earlier 4-4-0s, with a Belpaire firebox and Schmidt superheater. Unusually for an inside cylindered locomotive, No 341 was fitted with Walschaerts valve gear.

The engine's size and modern features excited attention in the technical press. The civil engineer also took a close interest as the weight and axle loading almost breached the limits then prevailing, and he insisted on the engine being weighed every six months. This experience was Maunsell's first confrontation with weight issues, as were to become so important when improving 4-4-0 Classes D and E on the SECR.

No 341 was powerful, effective, and well-liked by engine crews on the Dublin-Cork expresses. It is thought that more were planned but Maunsell's successor, EA Watson, had other ideas by developing a 4-6-0 design instead. Part of the story of the Irish 4-6-0s directly relates to Maunsell's continuing involvement in Irish locomotive affairs and will be discussed later.

After Maunsell left in late 1913 to take over at Ashford, No 341 became a victim of circumstance. In service its superior performance over Watson's larger 4-6-0 was to cause embarrassment. It thus became something of

Coey, assisted by Maunsell, tried various inside-cylindered options in seeking a successor to the venerable and numerous 0-6-0 Class 101 (that is J15 if you live over the water). These included a large 0-6-0, a 2-6-0 and a 4-6-0, none of which was very successful as they suffered from problematic weight distribution. The 4-6-0s were Classified 362 and totalled six; No 366 is at Glanmire Yard, Cork. When built in 1905, these were the largest engines in Ireland and the GS&WR was sufficiently proud of them to place one on display at the 1907 Dublin Exhibition. They were also the least successful of this generation of freight engines suffering from appalling vibration and they only survived until 1931; experienced drivers knew to place their dentures in their pocket before climbing aboard! These experiences gave Maunsell an insight into the difficulties of creating larger locomotives by "stretching" an existing concept rather than by starting the design process from scratch

an orphan with no one in authority showing it much interest. On grounds that it was uneconomic to replace the unique boiler then nearing the end of its useful working life, No 341 was withdrawn in 1928 to widespread criticism that this was premature treatment for such a useful locomotive.

In parallel with passenger locomotives, there was also a need for larger goods engines. Maunsell worked with Coey on the development of replacements for the standard goods type, the venerable Class 101 0-6-0 which dated from 1866 (known in England as the J15, its later Inchicore classification). As with the 4-4-0 fleet, enlargement of the traditional 0-6-0 was constrained by weight issues. Between 1903 and 1909, 27 locomotives in five classes appeared as part of the next generation. Three 0-6-0 types were introduced, one of which was converted to 2-6-0 to ease front-end weight problems. A further 2-6-0 class was built later; there was also an attempt at a 4-6-0 that was the least successful of this group.

These classes were entirely conventional with inside cylinders and round-topped boilers, and none offered the potential to become effective successors to Class 101. The lesson for Maunsell was that simple enlargement of existing concepts and the addition of leading wheels to bear increased weight would not be enough to produce a new generation of competent freight locomotives.

Once in charge, Maunsell set about designing a modern 0-6-0 and the first four of Class 257 appeared in late 1913, following his departure for Ashford, and another four arrived a year later with some minor modifications. All had round-topped boilers (Belpaire boilers were installed from 1931 onwards) but were fitted with 8" piston valves and superheaters from new, making them one of the earliest modestly-sized engines to be so equipped in these islands. They were deservedly successful and popular.

Apart from Class 101, which has always occupied a special position in Irish locomotive history, these Maunsell-designed 0-6-0s were the best of that wheel arrangement inherited by the Great Southern Railways on that company's formation in January 1925. They should have provided a template for further construction but were unfortunately ignored. There were two subsequent attempts (in 1929 and 1934) to produce successors to the 101s, and both were poor efforts of no great consequence. In contrast,

Class 355 totalled seven built as large 0-6-0s in 1903. Being front-end heavy, they were rebuilt as Moguls in 1907/8, and reasonable if unexciting engines resulted. No 356 is depicted here as rebuilt again in 1925 with superheated Belpaire boiler and modernised cab. In this process it also received a Bissel truck that extended the wheelbase by 1' 6". In 1952, No 356 was heavily modified by Oliver Bulleid as the guinea pig for his planned 0-6-6-0T turf burner. No 356 looked comical with sundry pipes and drums adorning the boiler, and was painted in overall silver livery. It undertook its experimental tasks satisfactorily and was then stored, not being withdrawn until 1957. The resultant Bulleid turf burner No CC1 was simpler and more effective than Southern Region Leader No 36001 but time by then had run out for unusual innovations with steam.

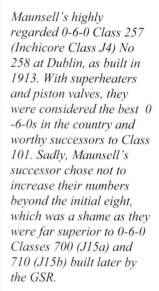

Maunsell's highly regarded 0-6-0 Class 257 (Inchicore Class J4) No 258 at Dublin, as built in 1913. With superheaters and piston valves, they were considered the best 0-6-0s in the country and worthy successors to Class 101. Sadly, Maunsell's successor chose not to increase their numbers beyond the initial eight, which was a shame as they were far superior to 0-6-0 Classes 700 (J15a) and 710 (J15b) built later by the GSR.

No 258 again, at the Broadstone, Dublin (ex MGWR) works on 23rd February 1960 with the Belpaire boiler that it had acquired in 1937. This class pre-dated the (English) Southern Railway 0-6-0 Class Q by 25 years, and two remained in service at Dublin after the last Q had been withdrawn.
JD Fitzgerald

the usefulness of Maunsell's engines was confirmed when No 264 became the first CIE engine to be converted to oil-firing in 1947.

Southern Class Q No 30535, the last in BR service, shunted at Salisbury until June 1965, despite official withdrawal the preceding April. Probably few British enthusiasts would then have realised that elsewhere there were two Maunsell 0-6-0s still at work – just. Class 257 Nos 261 and 262 were the last steam engines in service with CIE being withdrawn late 1965; the latter continued "in service" as a stationary boiler at Kingsbridge, Dublin into 1966.

Maunsell's short reign at Inchicore resulted in the construction of only one tank locomotive, an 0-4-2ST named *Sambo* for service as the Inchicore Works shunter. This was reputedly fabricated out of spare parts and although attributed to Maunsell, it was not completed until 1914. On the other hand, another tank locomotive design that did not get beyond the drawing board was relevant to later practice on both the SECR and the Southern

A type always scarce in Britain was the heavy locomotive built solely for shunting duties in the manner of

the American "switcher". By 1914, the British wagon population numbered about 1.3 million but as freight was moved in small wagons in relatively short trains, small locomotives usually sufficed. However in 1907, the Great Central Railway started a new method of operating at their two hump marshalling yards at Wath-upon-Dearne in Yorkshire. The tonnage processed was enormous but the use of only four locomotives to work these yards was unprecedented. Built by Beyer Peacock, they were purpose-designed 3-cylinder 0-8-4Ts (nicknamed "Daisies") that shared many dimensions with the GCR standard heavy goods 0-8-0 Class 8A (the "Tinies"). The three cylinders imparted steady, even torque yielding good control at slow speeds as the Daisies propelled long lines of wagons over the humps.

The need for only four was possible through the manner in which they were used. They worked continuously from 0001 hrs on Monday morning to 0600 hrs the following Sunday. Daily light servicing took place on weekdays between 1400 hrs and 1600 hrs; Sundays were devoted to more thorough attention. For a country with a history of profligacy in the construction and deployment of tank locomotives, the economy implicit in this operational intensity was striking.

It is not known to what extent Robinson and Maunsell had been in contact during their shared period in Ireland (1896 to 1901) but they must have surely known each within the local engineering community. Either through personal contact or by virtue of the publicity that attached to the 0-8-4Ts, Maunsell adapted the Daisy format in plans for a three cylinder 0-8-2T shunter, but this project stalled over difficulties in finding enough room for the inside valve motion. The problem could have been solved with Harry Holcroft's conjugated valve mechanism that was applied to overcome space limitations with the pioneer Gresley three cylinder engine, Great Northern 2-8-0 No 461. Ironically, Holcroft was later to work for Maunsell and would have been well-versed in what was required to make the 0-8-2T feasible.

As will be apparent from the drawing, the engine would have been smaller than the Daisies with proportionately reduced fuel and water capacities. This aspect would have alleviated an operational difficulty with the 0-8-4Ts arising from their continuous use over long shifts, necessitating carrying capacities for 3000 gallons of water and five tons of coal. Water is a dense substance and as levels reduced, the factor of adhesion dropped significantly leading to these mighty engines being prone to slipping in wet conditions.

The nature of the GS&WR's goods traffic was completely different from that of the GCR in Yorkshire so the need for such an engine might seem strange. However, the company handled vast exports of livestock to Britain through Dublin Docks. Cargoes on the hoof needed care when shunting and the even torque through 3-cylinder drive would have reduced discomfort to animals in transit.

Just as he chose not to expand on Maunsell's 4-4-0, his successor (EA Watson) abandoned the 0-8-2T idea in favour of a 2-cylinder 4-8-0T that employed many standard GS&WR components. The resultant No 900 appeared in 1915 and was an ungainly beast that derailed on sharper curves in Dublin's North Wall yards. This has been attributed to poor balancing with 28% of the adhesive weight (21% of the total weight) borne by the leading coupled axle. (Interestingly, derailments afflicted Urie's Class G16 4-8-0Ts at Feltham yard in their early days but for a different reason. It was discovered that several curves at this new facility had been laid to tighter radii than the stipulated minimum that the G16s had been designed to handle).

Thus by 1915 Maunsell had considered or would have become fully aware of the pros and cons of three wheel arrangements (0-8-4/ 4-8-0/ 0-8-2) possible in eight-coupled tank locomotives. His second attempt at a specialised shunter involved yet another – a two cylinder 2-8-0T on which design work started in mid-1918. Construction of six was authorised in July 1919 for use at Bricklayers Arms, Rochester and Ashford plus a pair for Hither Green where shunting was continuous on weekdays.

Selection of the unusual 2-8-0T wheel arrangement was presumably at the instigation of GH Pearson who had moved from Swindon to become Assistant CME at Ashford in 1914, and who was familiar with the formidable GWR Class 42xx. Pressure of work at Ashford led to deferment of construction and in the interval, the plans were modified to embrace three cylinders with Holcroft's conjugated valve gear. This proposal remained on the books until 1929 when it was cancelled in favour of the 3-cylinder 0-8-0T Class Z.

Thus Maunsell arrived at the optimal solution for a heavy shunter in the classic "switcher" vein by examination of five different wheel arrangements over more than 16 years. His last attempt at this specialised type was thus realised through a prolonged refinement and evaluation of

Four-cylinder Class 400 No 404 as built. In 1929/30, Nos 400, 404 and 408 were condemned as being no longer required. This decision meant that No 400 had a working life of 13 years while the other two would have worked for only seven years – extremely short lives by Irish standards. However No 404 had a curious history as personnel at this engine's home shed believed it to be the best of an indifferent bunch. Thus on local initiative and without any official sanction, the identity of No 404 was swapped with that of No 409. In 1935, No 404 now carrying the identity of No 409, was rebuilt with two cylinders in 1935 and stayed in service until 1958. Officialdom never knew of the masquerade – or so it was claimed.

Before Maunsell was asked to redesign No 402, sundry modifications were tried to improve the 400s. No 409 (withdrawn 1930 in the guise of No 404) was one of three (Nos 407-409) built by Armstrong Whitworth in 1923 in saturated condition, which predictably proved even worse than the superheated version. This was quickly corrected but a later, unsuccessful alteration was to install outside steam pipes as shown here, in the hope of improving the tortuous steam passages. These pipes were not lagged and some wags asserted that the resultant super-cooling was intended to offset any benefit that might derive from superheating.

the alternatives. Large shunting tanks present particular design challenges with the constraints presented by the British loading gauge, the need for maximum adhesion, the importance of weight distribution, and provision of sufficient room for coal and water. These combine to complicate the process of squeezing everything into the restricted volume afforded by a single carrying chassis.

Admiring Class Z on banking duties at Exeter many years later, it would have been hard to believe that they were the culmination of a design journey that had started in Dublin, influenced by unique operations commenced in Yorkshire in the 1900s. The omission of one of these machines from the preservation ranks is a tragedy not only for their inherent brilliance, but also because there is no surviving representative of a small but technically fascinating group of locomotives. The key weight-related dimensions of Class Z and its forbears appears below.

Maunsell's second spell at Inchicore was timely. The evolution of the 4-4-0 family identified limitations in traditional designs, and exposed him to key elements of 20th century steam – tapered boilers, Belpaire fireboxes superheating, Walschaerts valve gear and piston valves. This knowledge stood him in good stead but before he could apply it to his own designs, the Irish connection was to play a further, albeit regressive, role.

Joining the SECR and finding a locomotive department in disarray, Maunsell obtained engines and components from other railways as a temporary measure while assessing current construction plans. Unsure of the abilities of the Ashford team, he sent the drawings for the planned Class L 4-4-0 to Inchicore for appraisal. This led to removal of the complex spark arrester, deepening of the firebox, and installation of pop safety valves. Most significantly, the valve gear was modified with the valve lap shortened to 7/8". This dimension was favoured by EE Joynt, the Chief Draughtsman and was to be significant later for the GS&WR 4-6-0 family.

With the amended drawings to hand, the next problem was to get the new 4-4-0s built quickly. Ashford did not have spare capacity and of the British commercial builders, the best offer was from Beyer Peacock who could only guarantee production of twelve within 6 to 8 months. Maunsell then invited foreign builders to tender and Borsig of Berlin delivered another ten in June/ July 1914, literally on the eve of the Great War. This episode amply demonstrates his willingness to look beyond his immediate hearth for solutions.

An aspect of Maunsell's work in Ireland that was to be significant later in England was superheating, which was to become a contentious issue at Inchicore. The

Railway	GCR	GSWR	GSWR	SECR	Southern
Designer	Robinson	Maunsell	Watson	Maunsell	Maunsell
Class	8H	Proposed	900	Proposed	Z
Type	0-8-4T	0-8-2T	4-8-0T	2-8-0T	0-8-0T
Water capacity	3000 gallons	1500 gallon	1500 gallons	1200 gallons	1500 gallons
Coal capacity	5t 0c	c. 2t 10c	3t 10c	2t 15c	3t 0c
Max axle loading	18t 18c	2nd driver 16t 10c	1st driver 17t 4c	2nd driver 18t 0c	All drivers 17t 18c
Adhesive weight	75t 12c	65t 0c	62t 9 c	2-cyl 69t 7c	71t 12c
Total weight	99t 0c	77t 0c	80t 15c	2-cyl 77t 11c 3-cyl 80t 5c	71t 12c
% Adhesive/ total weight	76%	84%	77%	2-cyl - 89%	100%

The rebuilding of the unsatisfactory 4-cylinder 4-6-0 Class 400 with two cylinders was a complex story. The first so treated was No 402 in 1927 according to plans prepared by Maunsell at the request of JR Bazin, CME of the GSR. The actual design work was undertaken by Harry Holcroft who had moved to Ashford from Swindon. The result retained only the original driving wheels, boiler and tender; no other Class 400s were so extensively rebuilt. No 402, always readily identifiable among the 2-cylinder engines by its unique straight running plate over the driving wheels and cylinders, was considered the best of the class. On rebuilding, it was re-classified Class 402 (also B2a under the little used "Inchicore" classification system). Maunsell was closely associated with 4-6-0s on the English Southern Railway but No 402 was possibly the best of this wheel arrangement attributed to him.
Real Photographs Co Ltd

Schmidt superheater on 4-4-0 No 341 had convinced him of the advantages, but it could suffer from steam leakages. To eliminate this problem, and to avoid further royalties, Maunsell initiated his own form of superheater for use with his Class 257 0-6-0s. The first four carried Schmidt superheaters but the new type was ready for installation in the second batch (Nos 261 to 264) completed in late 1914, after his departure to Ashford. The actual design work was undertaken by his assistant Hutchinson, who was holder of the patent.

Maunsell's successor (Watson) did not exploit the Hutchinson superheater beyond these four engines but instead set about developing his own form of superheater, which proved less effective than the Schmidt type. This experience might well have influenced his successor, JR Bazin, who was reluctant over superheating generally, especially with smaller engines. It should be noted that others were busy developing their own designs around this time – notably Robinson, Churchward, Gresley, Hughes and Urie. In response, Dr Schmidt was planning legal action for breach of intellectual property rights but World War 1 put paid to such action. Schmidt's company apparently ceased operation about 1920 and he died in 1924 with nothing further of a legal nature transpiring.

The important outcome was that Hutchinson's design became known as the Maunsell superheater. It eliminated the leakage problem that had plagued the Schmidt type and was fabricated in such fashion that it was easy to service with excellent accessibility to all the key parts – a constant hallmark of the Maunsell engineering style. The superheater that therefore made its debut on GS&WR 0-6-0 No 261 went on to be extensively applied by the SECR and Southern.

The Inchicore period was also instructive in an engineering management sense. While traffic density was substantially lower than in Britain, Maunsell had to cope with financial constraints that had parallels with factors later in his career. Beyond the Dublin-Cork mainline much of the GS&WR network was subject to significant weight restrictions and permanent way quality was poor in certain areas. He therefore had to deal with the challenge of extracting maximum power from small locomotives against severe limits imposed by the civil engineer.

Also, by English standards the GS&WR was not wealthy, and finances were to be even more stretched for its successor, the Great Southern Railways. During his time with the GS&WR, and his later involvement with the GSR, Maunsell would have become familiar with the difficulties of steam fleet maintenance on a shoestring. The (English) Southern Railway was financially well-off but the electrification programme drained investment capital that would otherwise have been available for steam power; Maunsell's Irish experiences thus equipped him to work under such limitations.

Post-1913 influence at Inchicore

The 4-6-0s

A feature of Irish steam was variety. At its formation, the GSR mustered a fleet of 570 locomotives in 124 distinct classes; there were also significant variations and

Class 400 Nos 401 and 406 were rebuilt with two cylinders and Beardmore-Caprotti rotary cam valve gear in 1930 at a cost per locomotive of £7,000. It is believed that the manufacturers bore all or most of this expense as a sales promotion. In service, neither engine was considered as good as Maunsell's No 402. This posed the question whether the theoretical advantages of rotary cam valve gear could be translated into practical performance capable of matching, let alone exceeding, that of a well-designed conventional engine. In strict investment terms this expensive mid-life rebuilding was not viable. No 401 was rebuilt again in 1949 with outside Walschaerts valve gear to provide spare parts for No 406. In its final form it resembled the other four survivors (Nos 403/ 5/ 7/ 9) which were less comprehensive re-creations of No 402, and not so effective. On first rebuilding, Nos 401 & 406 were confusingly re-classified as Class 402 (B2a) although displaying prominent visual and technical differences.   *Real Photographs Co Ltd*

modifications that yielded a number of sub-classifications. The 4-6-0 fleet of the GS&WR/ GSR totalled only 22 yet abided by this tradition. By 1940, there were six with two inside cylinders (freight Class 362); ten with four cylinders (Class 400 as originally built); ten with two outside cylinders (three of Class 500 plus seven of Class 400 as rebuilt); and three with three cylinders (Class 800). In the context of 4-6-0s, Maunsell's name is usually associated with Lord Nelsons, King Arthurs etc, but this overlooks his varying degree of involvement with these Irish examples.

Class 362 was introduced during his term as Works Manager and this type's manifest shortcomings cogently identified that larger locomotives required more creative input than just simple stretching of an existing design. The next 4-6-0 type was Class 400 and in its original form was only a little more successful. Its arrival in 1916 was to have a profound impact on Irish locomotive practice, and it would be 21 years before the problems afflicting this design were finally eliminated.

Class 400 was the work of EA Watson, Maunsell's successor at Inchicore. He was Irish born but had spent most of his career overseas, initially in the United States and then as Assistant Works Manager at Swindon (between 1906 and 1911) with responsibility for carriage and wagon matters. This was unusual as Swindon typically exported rather than imported senior engineering personnel; he appears to have been engaged for his American workshop know-how.

Watson had been unpopular at Swindon and was apparently levered out, but nonetheless he managed to be appointed Works Manager with the GS&WR at the age of 30 years. How this happened is a mystery as his questionable engineering abilities were compounded by an arrogant and abrasive manner. The working harmony of the management team from the Coey/ Maunsell era soon evaporated in his dogmatic pursuit of a large engine policy. To widespread relief, Watson moved on from Inchicore in 1921 to become General Manager of Beyer Peacock. In so doing he left the GS&WR with a legacy of only two designs, both of which were viewed as sub-standard – the previously mentioned 4-8-0T heavy shunter and the 4 -cylinder 4-6-0 Class 400.

Watson had come to Ireland with a full set of drawings for the GWR Star Class, and a firm belief in the superiority of the Swindon school over all others. He also studied the London & North Western Claughtons in the design process. The 400s had outside Walschaerts valve gear with the inside valves actuated by rocking shafts i.e. the opposite of the Star layout. The parallel, superheated boilers had Belpaire fireboxes and a working pressure of 175 lbs/ sq in. They could run fast on occasions but were usually sluggish with a voracious appetite. The prototype was easily out-performed by Maunsell's 4-4-0 No 341 when it worked turn and turn about with No 400 on Dublin-Cork expresses. Such was Watson's unpopularity that it was alleged, but not substantiated, that he had No 341 negatively modified to reduce the embarrassment.

Despite the prototype's manifest shortcomings, nine more were built between 1921 and 1923 – three at Inchicore (Nos 401/2/6) and six by Armstrong Whitworth (Nos 403-5, 407-9). The first six were slightly better than No 400 but still plagued with problems. Almost in desperation, the final three (407-409) were built as saturated engines with boiler pressure increased to 225 lbs/ sq in to compensate. In this state they were even worse than No 400, and were soon superheated with boiler pressure reduced to 175 lbs/ sq in.

The problems had several causes including tortuous steam passages and flimsy frame construction but performance was most acutely affected by valve design. EE Joynt (Chief Draughtsman), who was accustomed to the short lap tradition of the GS&WR 4-4-0s, resisted Watson's Swindon-derived views, and wished to adhere to ⅞". Despite their strained relationship, they eventually agreed on a compromise lap of 1¼" that was still significantly shorter than the Swindon standard of 1½ to 1⅞".

JR Bazin, who had started his career with the English GNR in 1897 as a premium apprentice to HA Ivatt, became Running Superintendent for the GSWR in 1921 and shortly thereafter succeeded Watson as CME. Accordingly he was immediately embroiled in the motive power crisis stemming directly from the flawed 400s. Difficulties were exacerbated by their being confined by size and weight to the Dublin-Cork line, preventing their transfer to less demanding duties. Further, the company's financial condition was parlous with a repair backlog from the Great War compounded by extensive damage to infrastructure and rolling stock sustained in the Irish Civil War.

Minor attempts to improve Class 400 achieved little and it was not until 1926 that a serious effort to remedy matters was possible. In the interim, the situation was eased by introduction of 2-cylinder 4-6-0 Class 500 of Bazin's design, ostensibly for mixed traffic work (the prototype in 1924 and two more in 1926). These had the Class 400 boiler with pressure increased to 180 lbs/ sq in and with a slight reduction in superheater area. Driving wheels of 5' 8½" were fitted and they proved thoroughly competent machines, even on express services. The assembly of kits of 2-6-0s purchased from the UK and introduced into service from 1925 also eased the motive power crisis.

Class 500 used 1½" lap valves but it is unclear whether this was on advice from Maunsell or as a copy of Gresley's pioneer K3 2-6-0 No 1000. The long lap used on the K3 seems to have been coincidental, given that the LNER had yet to learn the crucial message delivered by GWR No 4079 during the 1925 Locomotive Exchanges. On the other hand, Maunsell had by then fully embraced the long lap principle, based on evidence provided by his assistant Pearson. (Despite the short lap guidance provided

Maunsell's only 0-4-2ST was the numberless Sambo, reputedly built out of spare parts to serve as the Inchicore Works shunter (a four-coupled type was essential to negotiate tight curves in the works). It was GS&WR practice for small tank engines to carry names but no numbers. Other names included Elf, Imp, Fairy, Sprite, and Jumbo. Maunsell's Sambo had a long life, surviving as pilot at Amiens Street shed, the last bastion of steam in the Dublin area, until 1962.   EM Patterson

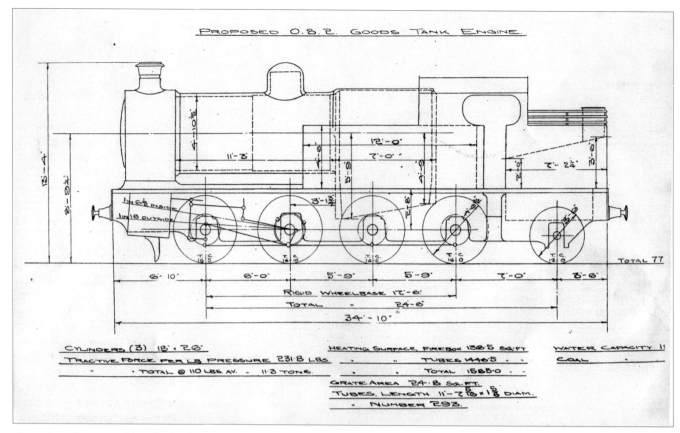

PROPOSED O.8.P. GOODS TANK ENGINE.

CYLINDERS (3) 18" × 26"
TRACTIVE FORCE PER LB PRESSURE 231.8 LBS.
" " TOTAL @ 110 LBS. AV. 11.3 TONS.

HEATING SURFACE, FIREBOX 138.5 SQ.FT
" " TUBES 1446.5 " "
" " TOTAL 1585.0 " "
GRATE AREA 24.8 SQ.FT.
TUBES, LENGTH 11'-7⅝" × 1⅝" DIAM.
" NUMBER 293.

WATER CAPACITY 1!
COAL .

Drawing of proposed 3-cylinder 0-8-2T. Although no direct connection has been traced, it is believed that the Great Central 0-8-4T Class 8H (LNER Class S1) heavy shunter was the inspiration for this project. The idea foundered because Maunsell was unable to work out a way of accommodating the valve gear for the inside cylinder within the limited space available. Ironically, Harry Holcroft who later worked for Maunsell at Ashford came up with a solution to this problem but of course it was then too late to be applied on the GS&WR.

Maunsell's plan for a 3-cylinder 0-8-2T heavy shunter having failed to materialise, his successor introduced No 900 as a 2-cylinder 4-8-0T in 1915. Extensive use was made of existing components and standard GS&WR dimensions but the end result did not look right, and was prone to derailment in Dublin's North Wall Yards. This was allegedly due to it being eight-coupled but as the driving wheelbase was shorter than that of the 0-6-0 Class 101, the more likely cause was a combination of excessive weight on the leading driving wheels and poorly laid track. Shortly before withdrawal in 1928, the rear coupling rods were removed and No 900 ran as a 4-6-2T but without any improvement. Maunsell continued to explore the heavy shunter concept after moving to Ashford. He was doubtless aware of this design's shortcomings, which provided potent evidence of how not to proceed.

by Joynt at Inchicore with the Class L of 1914, his next 4-4-0 was the excellent Class E1 of 1919 with 10" piston valves and 1 5/8" lap).

The Class 400 resuscitation programme commenced when Bazin sent a full set of drawings to Maunsell at Ashford in 1926 with a request for help. The challenge was passed to Harry Holcroft who designed what amounted to a new locomotive. This retained the boiler and driving wheels but had new frames, modified wheelbase, and two cylinders with outside Walschaerts valve gear. The boiler pressure was raised to 180 lbs/ sq in, and the new cylinders were 19½" x 28" with 10" piston valves. Crucially, the valve lap was increased to 1½".

Only No 402 was rebuilt in this fashion and while details have not been traced, the process must have been expensive. Before more engines could be similarly treated, William Beardmore & Co stepped in with an offer to rebuild two of the class with two cylinders and Beardmore-Caprotti valve gear. Nos 401 and 406 were chosen in an exercise that retained the original frames; the reported cost was £14,000, a staggering sum for those days. It is believed that most or all of this expense was borne by Beardmores who were actively promoting poppet valves to help consolidate their recent entry into commercial locomotive construction. Of the remaining 400s, three were scrapped in 1929/ 1930 and the other four were given a cheaper version of the 402 rebuild, retaining the original frames and the 1¼" valve lap.

During the 1920s, there was an emerging belief that poppet valves offered a significant advance over traditional piston valves, so comparison of No 402 with Nos 401/ 406 allowed the opportunity to assess the relative merits. Over the years No 402 was considered by locomotive crews as the best of the seven survivors with a consistent ability to out-perform the Caprotti engines.

By the time the last 4-cylinder Class 400 was being rebuilt, work had started on the final and most famous of the Irish 4-6-0s. The first of the three members of Class 800 (B1a), commonly but erroneously referred to as the "Queens", appeared in 1939. Much has been written about this legendary design and there was some mystery about its conception. Earlier classes introduced under GSR auspices were lacklustre and out-dated. On this form, the appearance of a modern 4-6-0 express engine that some have compared with the GWR's King Class was quite a surprise. The 800's had enormous publicity impact and symbolised a hopeful and progressive future for both the railway and the country at large.

In view of the earlier troubles with 4-6-0s, it is believed that EC Bredin who had taken over as CME in 1937 would not have risked producing such a ground-breaking machine without outside help. The design was substantially larger than anything that had gone before and unprecedented in the use of three cylinders. The only class in Ireland to that date with three cylinders was the GNR(I) Class V 4-4-0 compounds of 1932 which owed much to the English Midland 4-4-0s compounds, including the archaic 11/16" valve lap.

One outside source of technical advice was readily evident as Class 800 had streamlined steam passages in the manner ordained by Chapelon. However, regarding the rest of the layout the most likely source of help was Britain where operating conditions were broadly similar. Without firm information, identification of the most probable source is a matter of deduction. The GWR, with no experience of three cylinder designs, can be immediately discarded. Bazin with his LNER connections had retired in 1929 and there is no evidence of any further significant contact between the two companies. Further, the Belpaire firebox and three sets of Walschaerts valve gear owed nothing to Gresley practice.

The LMS has been cited as possibly having had a consultative role, a view that can be discounted given the

After looking into the 0-8-4T, 0-8-2T and 2-8-0T wheel arrangements, and being well aware of the problematic 4-8-0T, Maunsell eventually chose the 0-8-0T type which was manifest in the English Southern Railway's magnificent Class Z. Here No 30956 gives a hefty shove out of Exeter St David's up the 1 in 37 incline to Exeter Central. Real Photographs Co Ltd

In contrast to the troublesome Class 400, Bazin's 2-cylinder Class 500 proved excellent from the start. They were notable as being only the second initiative involving 2-cylinder 4-6-0s with outside Walschaerts valve gear in these islands. Intended as mixed traffic engines with 5' 8" driving wheels they proved excellent performers on Dublin-Cork expresses, which not for the last time proved that small driving wheels did not necessarily inhibit higher speeds. It is believed that Bazin consulted Gresley and/ or Maunsell in preparing this design, which used the Class 400 boiler. Only three of the class were built (No 500 in 1924 and Nos 501/2 in 1926). More were planned but rendered unnecessary by Maunsell's Woolwich Moguls. No 500 is seen departing Mallow on 15 June 1964. Mr CRH Wilson, one time Editor of The Locomotive, determined to build a high quality model of a premier steam engine of the 1920s and approached the CMEs of the Big Four with a request for General Arrangement drawings. None would co-operate so he then asked Bazin who was delighted to provide every assistance. Work started in 1929 on a model of No 500 in the scale of 1½" to the foot and it took about 12 years to complete. It is regarded as Britain's definitive locomotive model, and is apparently so perfect that no one has ever had the heart to steam it! It is presently in store at Birmingham Museum.
P Ward

situation on that railway in 1937-9. The Royal Scots in original form were in decline, and Stanier's 3-cylinder Jubilees were still problematic. The unique No 6170 *British Legion*, which bore an external resemblance to No 800, was a one-off rebuild of an unsuccessful high pressure compound machine, and had yet to prove itself. It is thus unlikely that Bredin would have turned to the LMS for help.

This left the Southern Railway and here the circumstances are persuasive, in view of Maunsell's continuing friendly relationship with Inchicore. His informal attendance at planning meetings could easily be imagined where his experience with the marvellous 3-cylinder "Schools" class would have been valued. If indeed this was the case, then there might have been a sense of fulfilment that experience derived from his final 4-4-0 was of help in the same offices where his first 4-4-0, GS&WR No 341, had been designed years before.

As a postscript to the design of Class 800, DL Bradley in *Locomotives of the Southern Railway Part 1* (RCTS 1975) commented *"...(the Schools) were without*

doubt the finest passenger locomotives designed by Maunsell, although as often occurred in the days of steam, this was by good fortune rather than intent." It might be presumptuous to challenge an authority of Bradley's stature but taking into account Maunsell's diverse involvement in the Irish locomotive scene over the preceding 30-odd years, it seems probable that rather more than luck contributed to the success of the Schools

There remains a final twist in the 4-6-0 tale. No 800 came to the attention of others across the water and in 1940, HG Ivatt led a small delegation to Inchicore. Travel to the neutral country was a sensitive matter and permission to enter was only granted after Ivatt revealed his Irish connections. The GSR was more welcoming and made No 801 *Macha* available for the delegation to "play with" on the Dublin-Cork route. No 801 had only recently been completed and had yet to enter normal service. The LMS personnel were impressed with the performance and this episode is thought to have influenced the rebuilding of the Royal Scots, which commenced in 1943. If Maunsell did

Visually speaking, the Maunsell presence in Ireland was most obvious with the Woolwich Moguls which derived directly from the SECR Class N, as with Class 372 (K1) No 378 depicted here. Twelve kits of parts were purchased by the Midland Great Western Railway in 1924 shortly before that company was absorbed into the Great Southern Railways, and fifteen more kits plus four spare boilers were purchased shortly afterwards. Twenty were assembled between 1925 and 1929 as Nos 372-391, with 5' 6" driving wheels. Apart from modification for the wider gauge and fitting of tablet exchange equipment on the tender, they looked like their more numerous English counterparts. Little changed during their long careers, they later received typical GSR smokebox doors as carried by 4-6-0 No 500, to the detriment of their good looks.

help in the design of No 800, then the saga became even more circular as his peripheral contribution to the resuscitation process would have echoed his assistance to the LMS in the 1920s when he lent Lord Nelson drawings to help in the planning of the original Royal Scots.

The 2-6-0s and 2-6-4Ts

At the creation of the Great Southern Railways in 1925, the GS&WR had only one 5' 8½" 4-6-0 in service (No 500) but was planning to build a further nine. In the event, only two more were constructed (in 1926) as the need for more of this excellent design was largely displaced by the Maunsell-designed 2-6-0 based on the SECR Class N.

The second largest constituent of the newly formed group was the Midland Great Western Railway whose Locomotive Superintendent, WH Morton, became Bazin's deputy on the GSR. Morton was English having joined the MGWR from Kitson in the early 1900s. He was a self-effacing and somewhat reticent individual who "carried" a weak engineering team for several years before rising to

Locomotive Superintendent in 1915. His mild manner disguised a competent and progressive engineering mind with an enthusiasm for superheating that directly contrasted with Bazin's caution. Significantly, he had a keen eye for a bargain.

Morton was active in the war surplus market and in the early 1920s made some keenly priced purchases of locomotive components, loco coal wagons and travelling cranes. His most spectacular deal took place in the closing months of the MGWR's independent existence when he ordered 12 of the SECR-designed Moguls (Class N) then being manufactured at the Woolwich Arsenal. They were delivered as kits of parts to that company's works at Broadstone, Dublin in early 1925.

Intended to be designated MGWR Class D2, the first was completed in April in that company's lined livery as No 49 for an official photograph. It was then re-painted in plain GSR overall grey and entered service as No 372. The proposed numerical suffix in the MGWR classification differed from established practice and posed the question what would have been Class D1. It is fairly certain that

Top - Class 393 (K1a) No 397 at Inchicore shed in March 1947, equipped as an oil burner. The final six Woolwich kits appeared as Nos 393 to 398 in 1930, and were fitted with 6' driving wheels as indicated by the shallow splashers. There was no direct English equivalent of this type, as it had Class U size driving wheels and Class N driving wheelbase. This engine has received the rather ugly GSR-style smokebox door, largely camouflaged by the white "target" which is repeated on the tender sides. The purpose was to advise signalmen that the engine was an oil burner that could be sent straight through, and not diverted into a loop for the arduous, back-breaking chore of "raking out" and rebuilding the fire. Oil burning equipment on such useful engines was very welcome. From 1940 onwards, the GSR had struggled with the unusual challenge of being almost totally reliant on coal-burning steam engines but without any coal to burn. Recourse was made to raw turf, timber, various doubtful substitute fuels, and a dubious anthracite dust officially known as "duff" (which often used cement dust as a binding agent, and with a leavening of sawdust). Duff mixed with pitch produced better combustion but clogged the tubes. The most popular alternative was briquetted (i.e. compacted), dried turf and so prized was this low calorific fuel that firemen took to hiding their allocations. GNR(I) engines on Belfast-Dublin services only ventured across the border with heavily laden tenders to ensure that they had enough to make it home where coal supplies, albeit of poor quality, did at least exist.

JM Robbins

Morton had intended six to have 6' driving wheels but this was over-ruled by Bazin. The first dozen thus appeared as Irish equivalents of the Southern's Class N.

Morton's influence led to the purchase by the GSR of 15 more locomotive kits plus four spare boilers, even before the first engine had been assembled. Performance on the road soon justified this confidence. Irish practice had been largely conservative and apart from No 500's performance, recent locomotive developments had been broadly unsuccessful. The Moguls, usually known as the "Woolwiches", were a revelation for their power output in relation to their modest size, amply demonstrating the possibilities of a well-thought out modern design. The first 20 kits were assembled as GSR Class K1 – Nos 372 to 383 at Broadstone (between 1925 and 1927) and Nos 384 to 391 at Inchicore (1928/ 9), following concentration of all new build activity there.

Maunsell's classic did have shortcomings, although not all were inherently the fault of the design. Modifications to accommodate the 5' 3" gauge were minimised, resulting in inadequate cross-bracing of the frames which increased maintenance costs and led to cracking later in life. Retention of the original cab was criticised by crews used to the more generous proportions of Irish footplates. They were also dirty locomotives to work, due to poorer quality coal and to the absence of smoke deflectors. Requests to fit this feature were ignored, despite Class 400 No 409 having been so equipped for a time during the early 1940s.

The Woolwiches were used on express passenger services and quite intensively worked by Irish standards. They tended to be moved to goods duties as their mileages built up thus fulfilling their intended mixed traffic role. Freight work revealed a deficiency in brake power. Although the UK engines had their brakes improved, no such effort was made in Ireland and this is regarded as the prime cause of a fatal accident in December 1955 at Cahir involving No 375 on a sugar beet train.

At an average price of approximately £2,000 per engine before cost of assembly and gauge modification, the moguls were excellent value. In 1929, Morton took over as CME following the retirement of Bazin, and there were distinctive features to his three-year tenure at Inchicore before his promotion to General Manager of the company. With the economy in decline, he introduced no new designs but strove to improve the existing fleet in difficult circumstances. He suspended the Class 400 rebuilding programme and solved the need for more competent goods locomotives by starting to superheat Class 101 0-6-0s (dating from 1866!). Eventually 67 were so fitted, at last providing the GSR with large numbers of "modern",

competent goods engines that were so needed. Further, he augmented the express fleet in 1930 by completing the final six Woolwich kits with 6' driving wheels – the version that he had apparently planned as Class D1 for the MGWR.

These engines were a little recognised variant of the Maunsell template. All the Irish Woolwiches had the driving wheelbase of 7' 3" + 8' 3" as used in the original Class N. However the 6' version differed from the Southern's Class U which had the 7' 3" + 7' 9" driving wheelbase inherited from the rebuilding of the Class K "River" 2-6-4Ts. Thus the large wheeled Irish Moguls (Class K1a Nos 393-398) were the equivalent of a Class N/ U hybrid.

Neither 5' 6" nor 6' driving wheel diameters were standard dimensions for either the GS&WR or the MGWR. Driving wheels thus formed a sub-plot in the Irish Woolwich story. One kit remained unassembled and this is ascribed to the phantom 392, a number never used in the GSR list. The wheels from this kit were diverted to Bazin's 2-6-2T Class P1 No 850 of 1928. This solitary machine was the GSR's only truly modern tank locomotive and Nigel Gresley, who was planning his Class V1/ V3 at the time, closely monitored its development.

Of the six 5' 6" wheelsets rendered surplus from Nos 393-398, five were used with 0-6-2T Class 670 (I3) of 1933. Together with No 850, they worked the Dublin-Bray suburban services; their wheels were large for sharply timed start-stop commuter duties between closely spaced stations – further evidence of the GSR's financial problems. As neither Inchicore nor the Broadstone locomotive works could cast 6' driving wheels, it is thought that the bargain-conscious Morton negotiated with Maunsell for suitable wheels, either with his 1924 plans or when he took over in 1929.

The Woolwiches became the mainstay of GSR mainline power on all but the principal Dublin-Cork expresses. Their usefulness was enhanced by their availability for work over the ex-MGWR mainline to Galway and also the Rosslare-Waterford line, both of which were barred to the 4-6-0s. They even occasionally hauled (at reduced speed) excursion trains over the Dublin & Southern Eastern line to and from Bray in County Wicklow. Their nadir was during the Second World War, known as the "Emergency" in Ireland, when supplies of reasonable quality coal were non-existent. Operating the GSR during those years was a story in itself. Various fuel substitutes of doubtful quality were tried, and heavy delays became the norm as trains were side-tracked for fireboxes to be raked out and fires rebuilt from scratch. There is a story, perhaps apocryphal, of a train that took three days to cover the 165

Opposite bottom - *The GSR tried to develop tank engines for suburban services between Dublin and Bray, and Maunsell's involvement in this exercise was only peripheral. Class 850 (P1) of 1927 used 5' 6" driving wheels surplus from Woolwich Mogul kits. This solitary 2-6-2T was the GSR's only truly modern tank engine and not very successful. No 850's development was closely monitored by Bazin's erstwhile colleague, Nigel Gresley, who was planning his class V1 2-6-2T at the time.*

GB Seymour

Compared with No 850, the five-strong 0-6-2T Class 670 (I3) of 1933 was regressive. Again, the Maunsell influence was restricted to use of surplus 5' 6" driving wheels. It was evidence of the GSR's stretched financial condition that such large driving wheels should be used for engines on tightly timed suburban services with frequent starts and stops.

EM Patterson

miles from Dublin to Cork, so poor was the "fuel".

The Swindon-inspired fireboxes did not take kindly to this treatment. In the immediate post-war period with coal still in short supply but fuel oil by then available, 16 of the Class 372 and all of Class 393 were converted to weir-type oil-burners in 1947-8. The Woolwiches were by far the largest group of engines to be converted in a successful programme that was proportionately more comprehensive than that in Britain. Unfortunately it was of similar limited duration for the same reason – shortage of foreign exchange to pay for fuel sourced from outside the Sterling Area.

The GSR, nationalised as part of Córas Iompair Éireann in January 1945, faced severe difficulties throughout the 1940s with an ageing fleet that had been only partly rationalised. The comparatively large numbers of Woolwiches and their relative youth made them doubly useful, pending dieselisation. However, the early diesel electrics were plagued with problems so steam had to soldier on longer than planned. Class 393 disappeared between 1954 and 1959 while the more useful smaller-wheeled version was retired between 1955 and 1962.

Individual withdrawal decisions were largely determined by frame condition as cracking became prevalent. This echoed the experience with Classes N and U in their declining years but with the Irish contingent, there was to be no frame replacement programme. After CIE steam had ceased and Inchicore was clearing out surplus material, the pristine frames for the phantom No 392 were discovered under a pile of rubbish. If their existence had been known earlier, the working life of one of the Woolwiches might have been extended at modest cost.

There was yet another Irish locomotive family that could trace its lineage back to Maunsell's influence. Towards the end of World War 1 with uncertainty about the future structure of the railway industry, the Association of Railway Locomotive Engineers commenced work on designs suitable for use nationally. Maunsell, Churchward and Fowler led this project and before it came to a halt, the SECR 2-6-0 had been accepted, with some reservations, as the template for the ARLE standard Mogul. As might be expected, the Midland Railway had a dissenting view based on aversion to the long lap valves favoured by Churchward and Maunsell. In an unsuccessful attempt to persuade Derby, Ashford Drawing Office produced drawings and calculations supporting the modern valve design.

In 1926, a young draughtsman at Derby was

GSR Class 800 (B1a) introduced in 1939 were the largest steam locomotives in Ireland. They were three cylinder simples, yet another variant in the range of Irish 4-6-0s. Previous GSR designs had been uninspired so this class caused a great sensation that was redoubled when its considerable performance characteristics became apparent. Internal steam passages were to Chapelon's principles but by process of deduction, it is believed that Maunsell had a consultative role in planning the design, based on his experience with the Schools Class. The careers of Class 800 were curtailed by acute fuel shortages between late 1940 and 1948, and soon thereafter they were replaced on top-line duties by diesel power. No 801 Macha as shown here held a special place in railway history. In 1940, before its release to traffic, it was lent to a delegation from the LMS led by HG Ivatt for the visitors to play with on the Dublin-Cork route. The favourable impressions gained are believed to have contributed to the rebuilding from 1943 onwards of the Royal Scots, which assumed more than a passing resemblance to the 800s.

charged with the task of designing a new 2-6-4T and in the process he referred to the ARLE-approved 2-6-0 design, and to the Ashford-sourced drawings and calculations. His work received the support of the Deputy Chief Draughtsman (an ex-Furness Railway man) and the following year the "Fowler" 2-6-4T appeared, having made it out under the wire with 1½" lap valves. These engines, together with the Hughes "Crabs", were arguably the most effective new designs during a dismal period in LMS locomotive history.

The short/ long lap debate was re-ignited in the early 1930s within the management team of the London Midland & Scottish Railway (Northern Counties Committee), the second largest railway in Northern Ireland. The rival merits of a 5' 3" version of the Midland Compound and a six coupled, long lap simple engine were hotly contested with the latter eventually prevailing. A

Mogul version of the Fowler 2-6-4T appeared in 1933 and by 1942 a total of 15 were in service. These sound machines (LMS NCC Class W) had 6' driving wheels and retained the front-end layout derived originally from Ashford, combined with the parallel boiler of the English LMS tank engine.

The LMS NCC was not a large system and the view formed after the war that it could be worked effectively with tank engines alone. Between 1947 and 1950, eighteen examples of 2-6-4T Class WT were introduced. These were tank versions of the 2-6-0 Class W and resembled their Fairburn 2-6-4T contemporaries except for their parallel boilers which were interchangeable with those of the Moguls. The Maunsell-inspired front end was retained and these engines, nicknamed "Jeeps" for their go-anywhere capabilities, were to fill a special place in steam history. While the Class W Moguls were withdrawn between 1956 and 1965, the Jeeps remained intact as a class until March 1969. They were the last steam locomotives in normal mainline service in these islands. No 4, which in October 1970 was the last to stop work is now preserved and a popular performer on enthusiast specials. Further, a complete spare set of Jeep driving wheels also survive and there are proposals afoot to build a new member of the class.

There the story of Maunsell's Irish Moguls and other descendants from SECR Class N might have ended but there was one more short chapter. In 1945 the newly formed CIE, despite its financial problems, evaluated options for a new generation of motive power. One proposal was to convert the Woolwiches to three cylinder 4-6-0s, and the outline drawing reveals a smaller form of Class 800 in which only the tender and 5' 6" driving wheels would have been retained. New frames were intended plus the Type K boiler that had made its debut with Class 400 in 1936. The term "rebuild" was thus not entirely appropriate and was presumably adopted as a ploy to avoid reference to what in reality would have been a new locomotive. Details are not quoted with the drawing but overall weight would have been in the region of Class 500, thereby limiting route availability. The use of three cylinders indicates satisfaction with the arrangement of Class 800 but in the post war era was an unnecessary luxury for a secondary locomotive. This proposal did not get very far and might well have caused the great man to raise his eyebrows, had he not died at Ashford the previous year.

There is a tendency to regard Richard Maunsell as perhaps less important than his Big Four contemporaries, for having constructed proportionately fewer steam locomotives. This would be a grossly unfair assessment as study of his work and achievements beyond the boundaries of the (English) Southern Railway reveal an engineer of international stature. His influence was profoundly important from his return to Inchicore in 1896 right through to the very end of Irish steam. Indeed, if a new LMS NCC 2-6-4T Class WT does appear one day then this will be yet another manifestation of his creative spirit.

LMS Northern Counties Committee 2-6-0 Class W traced its pedigree back to Maunsell's Class N, particularly in front end layout. Unnoticed by the ex-Midland Railway hierarchy at Derby, the "Fowler" 2-6-4T of 1927 was built with long lap valves (plus decent sized axle boxes) and a very good locomotive resulted. In turn, this was used as the basis for a new 2-6-0 for service in Northern Ireland of which No 94 The Maine was an earlier example, built in 1934. As with the Hughes "Crab" Moguls there was a disparity in width between the cab and the tender; later members of this fifteen strong class had small Stanier style tenders that suited their lines better.

LMS NCC 2-6-4T Class WT was introduced as a tank version of the Moguls, sharing the same parallel boiler. Known as "Jeeps" for their go-anywhere capability, this class of 18 locomotives remained intact until April 1965. No 51 as shown here was taken out of service in January 1970 and officially withdrawn in February 1971. No 4, the last steam locomotive in normal service in these islands finished work in October 1970, before starting a second very successful career in preservation. The owners of No 4 have in their possession a spare set of driving wheels and are considering building another example. If this project goes ahead then the story of Maunsell's legacy in Irish steam, however remotely connected, might not yet be ended.

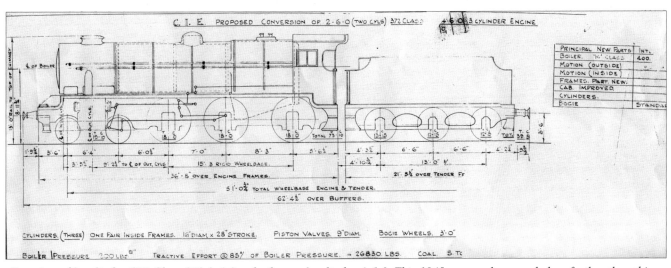

Drawing of 2-cylinder CIE Class 372 2-6-0, rebuilt as a 3 cylinder 4-6-0. This 1945 proposal proceeded no further than this stage.

REMEMBER THE 1950s?

REMEMBER THE 1950s?

Andrew Harris has kindly submitted a batch of photographs (plus a couple of articles for future use).

Variety there certainly is with (opposite top) D15 4-4-0 No 30464 at Waterloo on 28 June 1953. The engine was waiting to take the RCTS 25th Anniversary Special on the first leg of its trip to Salisbury - but was delayed by late arrival of the stock. The headboard had yet to be fitted. Opposite bottom - E1R No 32608 at Barnstaple Junction, 15 August 1953.

This page, top right and centre we have what some referred to as 'The Wonder Engine', more exactly an 800hp diesel-electric whose history could be traced back to its genus on the LMS in 1946. (The nickname reputedly came from comments by the locomotive department based on the question 'I wonder if it will go today?') It is seen here at Norwood Junction on 3 April 1954. the engine was based here from May 1952 to December 1954.

Bottom is an LNER V2 No 60908 passing Eastleigh with a Bournemouth line service at the time the Bulleid engines had been temporarily withdrawn. 17 May 1953.

"A foggy day in London Town". Typifying the post-war austerity and London's pre-Clean Air Act "smog" a 3SUB with SECR bodywork stands at Blackfriars, 18 December 1946.

Getty Images / Hulton Archive 3350863

The EPB Story Part 2:
The need for new Suburban Electric Trains
David Monk-Steel

(Part 1 appeared in SW20)

The need for new Suburban Electric Trains

Rolling Stock for electric trains

The London and South Western Railway electrification system used three-coach fixed formation motor sets which could be coupled in multiple to make six-car trains.

When the Southern Railway electrified the South Eastern lines (and eventually when the Central section was converted from A.C.) the same arrangement was adopted. To increase capacity a two-car un-motored trailer set was inserted into some of the trains to operate as eight cars. The two-car trailers had no driving cabs, and outside the peak hours trains were split up as an economy measure and numerous 'blind-ended' trains were left stabled at the buffer-stop ends of suburban stations or in sidings. Shunting with a blind end was also common, and fraught with difficulty and danger.

How the original stock was formed

The rolling stock for these schemes indicated the Southern Railway Co's. policy of thrift and ingenuity. This was a clever initiative by the Southern Railway who were keen on re-cycling. The quantity of brand-new electric carriages was quite small, limited to 29 three-car units for the Eastern Section (Victoria to Orpington lines) and 26 sets for the Western Section. This stock was ordered from and built by Metro Cammell. All the rest of the 'new' sets were in fact reconstituted steam stock.

The reconstituted sets followed a policy originated on the London and South Western whereby steam-hauled suburban stock was taken into works and converted to electric operation. Most of the new stock was mounted on brand-new 62-foot-long underframes but the bodywork was taken from former South Eastern, London and South Western or London Brighton and South Coast 4- and 6-wheeled carriages. The South Eastern & London and South Western carriages were similar in profile with elliptical roofs and panelled sides, but the London Brighton and South Coast carriages had arc roofs, and looked quite different. The new underframes are to feature in the EPB story, as the policy of re-cycling did not finish here, but that is for another chapter. The method of construction involved removing the original wooden bodywork from short frames, and assembling the resultant kit of compartments as convenient until the new frame was filled. Any gaps were panelled over, leading to further variation within sets. Certain brake vehicles were given driving compartments and control equipment, together with the necessary current collection gear and traction motors. Intermediate cars were given cabling for control, and all cars were air-braked. The cab ends were new; usually steel sheet panelling over new timber framing. Cab roof ends (only) were domed

The sets were initially assembled into three-car motor sets and two-car trailer sets, but for a short period some of the new sets were formed of two motor cars and two intermediate cars, but as the first class accommodation was situated in the intermediate cars this gave an imbalance of accommodation. Sets varied, but a typical three-car set would seat 240/250 persons, (of which about 75 were first

Grove Park on the first day of public electric service, 28 February 1926. Three former South Eastern lines had commenced an electric service on that day, from Charing Cross and Cannon Street to Orpington, Bromley North, Addiscombe and Hayes. The intention had been to introduce the service on 1 December 1925, but power supply difficulties had prevented this.

3SUB set No. 1709 probably on a Waterloo to Waterloo via Hounslow and Richmond loop service. The LBSC bodywork with its characteristic single-arc roof is clearly seen in this low-level shot.

class!) and a three + two + three train could seat about 650 persons with many more standing in acute discomfort. A survey immediately post-war discovered 1,800 persons travelling in one train alone.

Three-car motor sets and two-car trailer sets were ordered for each electrification scheme as it was authorised and the following is a summary of the electrification schemes and the stock ordered for each. Once delivered however the trains entered the general pool of sets and no attempt was made to keep them on the lines for which they were originally ordered.

The Three-Car Motor Sets

Eighty-four sets were originally built for the London and South Western Railway for use on Waterloo to Kingston, Shepperton, Hampton Court and Claygate services, and Metro Cammell built 26 more for the Southern Railway for extensions to those services to Guildford and Dorking.

In 1925 the Southern Railway converted various former South Eastern Railway's coaches into 95 three-car sets for use on Victoria to Orpington, Charing Cross/Cannon Street to Dartford and Mid-Kent services and purchased new from Metro Cammell 29 to a similar design for use on Victoria to Orpington services.

In 1926 they converted former South Eastern 4-wheel and 6-wheel 'block' sets on new 62' underframes into 10 three-car

sets for use on Charing Cross, Charing Cross/Cannon Street to Dartford and Mid-Kent services and also, later on, the London Bridge to Caterham and Tadworth Services.

30 more from the same source were converted in 1928 for the extension of the electrification to the Central Section and the conversion of the A.C. lines to D.C. At the same time 42 three-car sets were formed from former London Brighton and South Coast Railway bogie 'block' sets on new 62' underframes, and 44 three-car sets were created from former London and South Western Railway bogie 'block' sets on new 62' underframes,

The A.C. electric sets thrown up spare by the conversion were themselves adapted to make 56 three-car sets in 1928/1929 particularly for the Dorking to Sutton, Wimbledon to Sutton and for service enhancements. However they were used indiscriminately on all S.R. Suburban Electric lines. These were not put on extended underframes.

Introduced in 1930 for the Dartford to Gravesend, Hounslow and Windsor services' extensions, a further 13 three-car sets were created from former London and South Western Railway bogie 'Block' sets. Inevitably they were used indiscriminately on all S.R. Suburban Electric lines.

More former London and South Western Railway bogie 'block' sets were put on new 62' underframes for service enhancements in 1931 creating 11 more sets, and were followed by five more sets created from former A.C. stock.

Introduced in 1934 / 5 for extensions to Sevenoaks, Sanderstead and for service enhancements, 15 more three-car sets were created when more former London and South Western Railway bogie 'block' sets were put on new 62' underframes. In 1937 a further six sets were created from former London and South Western Railway bogie 'block' sets on new 62' underframes for train service extensions to Staines and Weybridge and for service enhancements. Once more these were all used indiscriminately on all S.R. Suburban Electric lines.

On 31st August 1939 there were officially 466 three-car motor sets in stock. (423 required for service)

Two-car Trailer Sets

The two-coach trailer sets were formed exclusively of former steam-hauled coaches, originating from all three constituent companies, and there was considerable variety of seating and coach profile as a result. There were even sets containing coaches from different companies. There was a considerable amount of reforming and therefore the following can only be taken as an overall guide.

The London and South Western Railway first introduced 24 trailer sets in 1920. They were formed from steam-hauled 8-compartment third (formerly composite) carriages.

3SUB No. 1435 with SECR bodywork carrying an Eastern Section headcode on what appears to be an off-peak service.
WJ Wyse / Mike Morant collection

3Sub unit No 1528 at Otford on a Sevennoaks service. This was one of 135 3-car units introduced between 1925 and 1928 using recovered bodywork dating back to SECR days.

Southern Railway / David Monk-Steel collection.

80 two-car sets were introduced in 1925 by S.R., converted from pairs of London Brighton and South Coast Railway steam-hauled 9-compartment third stock,

55 sets were introduced in 1928 by S.R., converted from a former South Eastern Railway's steam-hauled 8-compartment coach coupled to former London and South Western Railway 6-wheel compartment third mounted in pairs on new underframes,

13 trailer sets were introduced 1929 / 1930, from pairs of former London Brighton and South Coast Railway A.C. "CP" electric motor cars.

Eight sets were formed in 1930, converted from a former South Eastern Railway steam-hauled 8-compartment coach (one set had a 9-compartment SEC coach instead) coupled to former London and South Western Railway 6-wheel compartment thirds mounted in pairs on new underframes.

Six more were introduced in 1930 / 1931, from former London Brighton and South Coast Railway AC electric trailer thirds (one 8½-compartment, and one 9-compartment)

Six sets were introduced in 1934, formed from pairs of former London and South Western Railway lengthened 10-compartment thirds, formerly 8-compartment, on new frames, reformed in 1937 with ex-London Brighton and South Coast Railway 9-compartment steam thirds.

The situation with trailer sets was always fairly fluid with frequent renumbering and re-formation. On 31st August 1939 there were officially 212 two-car trailer sets in stock.

The total suburban fleet

The Southern had 2002 suburban electric carriages at the start of World War 2, but all of it inherited some of the faults of the original steam stock from which it had been rebuilt: they could seat only ten persons in each compartment, and the mix of first and third classes meant that the space available in peak times, was not as efficiently used as it might be. Passenger comfort at busy times was also a great source of dissatisfaction. Nearly all the carriages in the three-car motor sets were mounted on new 62' underframes, even the original 84 London and South Western Railway motor sets had been given 62' underframes between 1935 and 1940, leaving a small number of former A.C. electric carriages, and the 23 sets supplied by Metro Cammell still on shorter underframes. The trailer sets were, however, a very motley collection of carriages, few of them were on long underframes, and many were in a poor state of repair.

Three-car to Four-car Augmentation

All the suburban stock (except for the 2-NOLs, which were really main line stock, and a few oddments used on the South London and Wimbledon to West Croydon lines of the former London Brighton and South Coast Railway.) consisted of three-car, compartment motor sets operating either singly or as six-car twins, strengthened during peak times with two-car compartment trailer sets inserted between. The operation of these blind-ended trailer sets was dangerous and complicated, so in 1942, the Southern Railway, no doubt spurred on by the additional operating difficulties caused by the blackout, and to avoid leaving coaches standing at the buffers of terminal stations during air raids, started reforming the three-car sets into four-car sets with trailer coaches removed from disbanded trailer sets, or from war-damaged motor sets. The de-classification of First to Third class no doubt also helped this process, as most trailer cars in the motor sets were composites.

Accidents and the call for 'all-steel' stock

By 1939 it was clear that existing rolling stock capacity was inadequate, and the policy of make do and mend was creating its own problems as 40 year old carriage bodies were showing their age and incapacity.

The press wase becoming increasingly aware and vociferous about the inadequacies of this old equipment, and a number of spectacular accidents (Purley Oaks, Battersea Park etc.) boosted public opinion calling for 'all steel' coaches to replace them.

New wide bodied (Six-a-side) rolling stock

New steam-hauled carriage stock introduced for the Bournemouth express services featured a new body profile, and it was soon realised that, by using this shape with new steel welding techniques, it would be possible to seat 12 persons in a suburban compartment even within the tight Eastern Section structure gauge, which increased the potential capacity of a carriage by nearly 20%. The Southern Railway carriage designers under O. V. S. Bulleid therefore conceived a four-coach suburban train on a 62' underframe with 11 compartments in one trailer carriage, ten in the other and nine each in the motor coaches, each seating 12 persons in various degrees of discomfort. An eight-car train of the new stock (Sets 4101 and 4102) could seat 936 persons, whereas an eight-car set of older wood-bodied stock could seat only 652. These figures are somewhat academic because during rush hours there might be as many people again standing, and with reduced 'leg' room in the new trains that number might be a lot less.

This was a simple development that might certainly put off the day when the infrastructure would have to be rebuilt at huge expense.

The new train didn't appear until after the war had broken out so the real value was not initially realised. Travel patterns changed drastically after 1940, as people were called up into the services, the city of London suffered damage from enemy air attack, and people remaining at work in London worked much longer hours. Rush hour travelling was still an unpleasant experience, but wartime forced people to complain less openly; although they did grumble a great deal they tended to do this in private.

Although compatible electrically with the former suburban units, these trains represented a major improvement. The bodies contained a great deal more steel in their construction, and after the first ten, which had wooden roof panelling. they could be regarded as 'all-steel'. The new train operated between Orpington and Victoria almost exclusively at first, having been allocated a strict diagram. As the older units were reformed into four-car trains it is likely that this discipline broke down more and more frequently so that by the end of the war it was fairly unpredictable as to the number of carriages likely to turn up at any platform, despite the most complex of plans.

Simultaneously, identical trailer carriages were built as intermediate cars to strengthen more of the three car sets to four cars, as the supply of suitable trailer sets dried up. These were referred to as 'augmentation' trailers, and these too enter the EPB story later on.

Main Line and Semi-fast Electric Stock

Although not strictly part of the suburban story it is worth mentioning that the electric trains for the main line electrification to Hastings, Brighton, Bognor and Portsmouth were all new vehicles built to the latest Maunsell design, gangwayed, (within each set at first and later with gangway connectors at the outer ends too), with deep windows along the corridor side and with a lavatory available to a high proportion of passengers. Main line trains were made up from four- or six-car sets, and frequently ran as twelve-car trains. The semi-fast services to Alton, Reading and Maidstone all received new stock too, marshalled into two-car sets to similar designs but with no through gangways and, in later sets, less lavatory accommodation. For the Gillingham and Maidstone services the carriages were more utilitarian in design.

The only semi-fast sets not built new were a series of 'semi-fast' two-car sets classified '2-NOL', and which were former London and South Western Railway steam stock from a similar source to that used for the suburban trains. There was very little difference between the 2-NOL sets and the suburban units. Semi-fast and suburban units were able to operate in multiple with each other, and did so fairly often, which was something that was not possible between the main line stock and suburban units.

Post-war development by the Southern Railway

Trials continued with the new six-a-side train during the War but no new trains appeared until 1946.

The end of the War and demobilisation of the forces returned people to civilian employment and the increasing numbers of travellers brought back the misery of rush-hour travel once more, made worse by the arrears of maintenance and general decline brought about by the war. Six-a-side all-steel carriages were again only considered as a partial solution, but more drastic measures would be needed if the Southern Railway was to supply the demand anticipated.

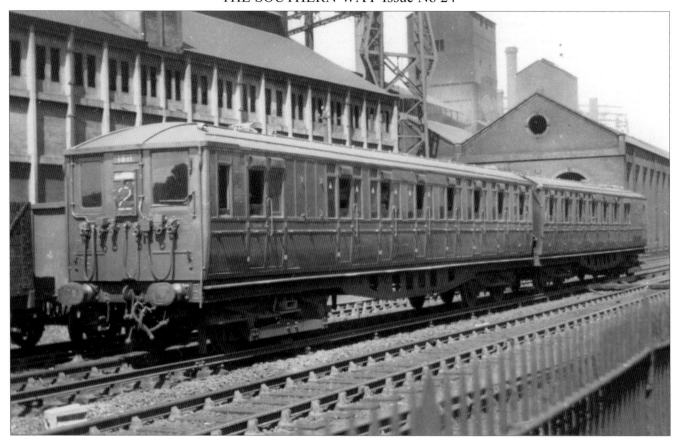

2WIM set No. 1811 passes Waddon Marsh Halt on a Wimbledon - West Croydon Line service. This Halt became part of the Croydon Tramlink in 1999/2000 and the site of the gasworks in the background became an Industrial Estate.

Various options were considered, and the strategy developed by the Southern hinged upon whether it was going to be more economic to renew the power supply system and lengthen platforms to accommodate ten carriages, or whether a more radical solution was to be used. In September 1931 the Southern Railway Magazine for staff published an article about a Roman (Italy, 1930s) tour bus which could carry 100 persons using a novel interlocking double deck system, and this must have struck a chord in the carriage drawing office, because a revolutionary four-car unit was designed which might usefully carry about 40% more passengers than the new six-a-side stock. This was to be known as the 'Double-Decker', which would overcome the need to extend the platforms at great expense, and to modernise the power supply also at great expense, and more of this will be told in chapter 3.

Until a decision had been made between Double-Deckers or Ten Cars the Southern Railway and the Southern Region of British Railways continued to turn out new 'all steel' four-car, six-a-side Westinghouse-braked units, most on new underframes, but as production continued, many started to appear on the underframes of the old three-car sets which were being withdrawn and which were barely 20 years old. The post-war design perpetuated a door to every compartment (or seating bay), but included a greater proportion of open saloon seating and the external appearance was considerably more austere than the older sets. These 227 sets were to be known as '4-SUBs', and lasted in service until the 1980s.

Eight more of the new six-a-side trains that were originally introduced in 1941 were added in 1945 following existing SR practice with canvas covered wooden roofs and a domed finish above the driver's cab. These units had much narrower compartments which, although they packed more passengers into the seats, were deemed to be much less comfortable, especially for standing passengers, than those that came after. Like the wooden-bodied stock numbered as sets 4101 to 4110 they acquired the nickname 'Sheba' suggested as a reference to the biblical Queen of Sheba who was reputed to have come to Jerusalem "with a very great train"!

Various batches followed in 1946, to a new all-steel design. Steel sheet panels supported by pressed steel sections welded into a single structure replaced the steel and timber hybrid construction of heretofore. All-compartment stock (sets 4111 to 4119) came first, followed by sets with various combinations of semi-saloon and compartments to gauge public reaction. The compartments were given greater width to accommodate a higher proportion of standing passengers in relative comfort, which remained an unfortunate feature of peak travel for the entire lifespan of 4-SUB and 4-EPB stock.

Unlike previous SR electric stock, the driving cab end was continued to the roof line without a dome, giving these sets a brutal slab-fronted appearance. The body was formed in a continuous curved profile and there was no discernible cant rail, the rain strip was positioned high on the sides of the roof and the body colour continued up to it. Each compartment had side doors with a small top light (or a lozenge shaped ventilator) above the droplight. The inner ends incorporated vertical pressed steel ribs to give structural rigidity. The motor coaches had a guard's compartment accessed by a double door, and the driving cab had an access door on each side as well as one into the guard's van. This basic body shape was to be perpetuated into the 4-EPB stock, which was built at Eastleigh on the same jigs. Sets delivered in this initial experimental phase included 4121 to 4130, and 4355 to 4377.

The 4-SUB unit design eventually standardised on a four-car formation with a driving motor brake saloon at the outer ends, with a compartment trailer, and a saloon trailer intermediately. Set numbers were 4277 to 4299, 4378 to 4387, 4601 to 4607 and 4621 to 4754. From unit 4621 onwards most of the driving motor coaches were erected on re-manufactured underframes recovered from withdrawn three-car units.

No two car suburban sets were built in this phase. The pre-war 2-NOL sets were used on specific working, chiefly between Waterloo and Windsor, or along the Sussex Coast lines, and there was a handful of two-car sets allocated to the South London line and the Wimbledon to West Croydon shuttle of 'Brighton AC' origin. The pre-war two-car trailer sets had either been scrapped or incorporated into the augmentation of the 3-SUB units to four cars. There was therefore no simple way of creating and operating ten-car suburban trains to accommodate the rising demand, especially on the Eastern section. For the time being eight-car working in the peak remained the norm.

A 1925-built Eastern Section unit augmented to 4SUB formation by the inclusion of an all-steel Bulleid trailer car.

REMEMBER LYMINGTON?

Opened as far back as July 1958 and extended to the Pier in 1884, the Lymington Branch had the distinction of being the last steam branch operated by BR, a steam shuttle between Brockenhurst and Lymington surviving almost to the end of steam working on the Southern in July 1967. On this and the next few pages we portray the station at Lymington Town as it appeared in the early 1960s.

At one time scheduled for closure under Dr Beeching, the branch survived and has since 1967 seen periods of both electric and diesel operation. In the view opposite top, there is a good indication of what were almost the total facilities, the approach from Brockenhurst made over a level crossing controlled by a signal box (see page 36) which was in use from 1928 until 1979, although from 1967 this had operated solely in the capacity of a ground frame. The run-round loop gave, at one end, access to the single road engine shed where coal and water were available, the former needing to be shovelled by hand to and from the coal stage seen. Two goods sidings, later extended to three, were provided on the opposite side of the line, one of these terminating within what was a commodious brick-built goods shed and one other having end-loading facilities.

The passenger station boasted an overall roof although sadly this was removed circa 1966 around the same time the goods shed was demolished and presumably goods facilities were withdrawn. Some siding removal occurred between March and May 1966 whilst further rationalisation saw the remaining siding, together with the run-round loop and engine shed taken out of use on 3 April 1967. Even so it was to be a further year before these items of track were removed.

The signal box, depicted on page 36, contained a frame of 25 levers. Tyers No 6 tablet was in use between Lymington Junction on the main line and Lymington Town until 3 April 1967. Between the Town and Pier operation was by train staff. The complete branch came under 'One engine in steam' operation from 3 April 1967, somewhat ironic as this was also the day the electric service started running.

What was left is what is now deemed to be a 'basic railway', a single line without turnouts of any sort running through to Lymington Pier. (Here too rationalisation had occurred leaving just a single line to a slightly repositioned platform.)

All Peter Elliott

A solitary covered van together with a Scammel 'Scarab', and trailer and p/way trolley are the only occupants of the yard. The signal box controlled the gates until 18 November 1979 when CCTV operated from Brockenhurst panel was commissioned. The siding at the rear of the signal box was the continuation of the goods shed road.

No 34071 '601 Squadron' cautiously setting off from the Ocean Terminal for Waterloo under the supervision of a somewhat stern looking railwayman.

TICKET CLERK - SOUTHAMPTON DOCKS
TONY CARTER

I had been working in ticket offices in Sussex which were very busy with hundreds of season-ticket-holders, in addition to being responsible for parcels in and out. There could not have been a greater contrast when I transferred to Southampton Terminus in the mid-1950s. Immediately of note was that the booking office here did not deal with either public enquiries or parcels traffic and there were virtually no season-tickets issued. Similarly there was no busy period and instead we two clerks worked alternate early and late shifts assisted by a day shift Chief Clerk. Outside there was a large station staff consisting of the Station Master's clerks (there was more than one), parcels clerks, station inspectors, ticket collectors, porters, cleaners, shunters, signalmen and guards.

The passenger train service was a hotch-potch assortment, with one train direct to Waterloo each way, plus cross-country workings to Didcot and also Cheltenham. Locally there were numerous short distance workings, mainly to Alton, Winchester and Eastleigh. Parcels workings were numerous and included services from the Western Region at Reading. The station would also briefly spring to life when the up and down Weymouth mail trains arrived about 12.30am. At first, we had a Sunday service, but this ceased in the late 1950s. When the Hampshire diesel services came along, we had a regular week-day local service but any increase in traffic was negligible so far as our station was concerned.

Local residents called the Terminus station by its old name of 'So'ton Docks', but any use of this name to non-locals was apt to cause confusion: as for example the Channel Islands boat train was advertised to the public as a service train arriving at 07.00 Sunday; but boat passengers would then have to purchase their ferry ticket from the Terminus station. The time taken for this after the arrival of the train plus the subsequent walk into the docks meant that some would usually miss the boat. (In the reverse direction their tickets included the journey to London.)

In the quiet times, of which there were many, we spent much of our spare time composing fare books for use as and when we needed them within the Docks. The Chief Clerk would help out at a ticket window but he was the one who would also go to the bank (without being missed) and in addition carry out the important task of emptying the lavatory locks of pennies. This was the only station I know where more cash was taken in the 'Gents' than the 'Ladies' – most of our customers (the word seems appropriate here) were male dock workers. The station itself had suffered much from bombing in the war and part of the upper storey of the South Western House, previously a Hotel, was then the headquarters of the railway's Marine Department.

In addition to station work, the clerks, parcel staff and ticket collectors regularly had to be in the docks to deal with passengers arriving off the various liners. These might arrive at night but only disembark after 8 am, times also dictated by the tides. Vessels were similarly frequently delayed by gales or fog. Their arrival times could not be guaranteed, so it was also hard to predict when we might finish duty. The latest I arrived home was at 1.30 am on one occasion.

USA 0-6-0T No 30062 with an RCTS railtour alongside the Ocean terminal building. Notwithstanding much in the way of records for special workings in the 1960s, it has not been possible to ascertain the use of this particular engine on an RCTS special. The conclusion is that is may have been a substitute engine.

43

The concourse at Southampton Terminus.

From a clerical perspective, the chief clerk had first call for dock duties, but the window clerks were used on an overtime basis and often relief clerks were also called in. When working in the docks, it was necessary to prepare cases of necessary items in advance: it just was not possible to come back to replenish. We would take change, trays of tickets, rubber stamps and ink pad, plenty of scrap paper, paper tickets books, scissors, rubber bands etc. The trays of tickets comprised two sets of 1st and 2nd class London singles, ten or a dozen printed single tickets to other principal destinations - plus blank cards to be written out for other stations and of course the fare books. Weather and tides would invariably affect more than one boat so several might arrive together, hence there were three other sets containing similar items. We had to gauge which boat would be busiest and would require the more comprehensive set of tickets. Issuing return tickets was virtually unknown as almost everyone was finishing their journey.

It also wasn't always the case that the biggest ships were likely to be the busiest, as on these many people might have bought tickets in advance through agencies abroad; hence experience came into play.

The railway charged boat train passengers a dearer fare so all our fare books had to list two sets of fares and, of course, this was reflected on every destination where a break of journey via London was involved.

There was a number of booked pathways available for boat trains shown in the working timetable and a 'Conditional' circular would come out the day before, advising signal-boxes en route which pathways would be used, although again these might be subject to last minute change if the ship was delayed.

Should a vessel arrive late in the evening, passengers might be offered the alternative of a service that night or early the next morning. Should there be only a handful of passengers disembarking, a single coach would be provided which was then worked round to Southampton Central to be attached to the next Waterloo train - not necessarily a very fast service although the passengers were still charged boat train rates. Easiest for us was when a ship tied up at the Ocean Terminal. Here were two purpose built ticket-offices each with a comprehensive set of tickets readily available.

In other cases, each of our portable trays would hold perhaps ten or twelve to a particular destination, each secured in an elastic band with a face card saying, for example, 'Birmingham', and the fare. For easy reference the price for 1, 1½, 2, 2½ or 3 passengers (the half being a child) was also given. On occasion and when particularly heavy bookings might be expected, we went on board the ship but then there was a rush to get off ahead of the public. Other than when using the Ocean Terminal, our ticket kiosk was invariably in a customs shed. Most were dark and gloomy places to work.

We would accept travellers' cheques (sterling or other currencies) plus bank notes from the USA, Canada, Australia and New Zealand - each having a different exchange rate. For simplicity, we used a fixed exchange rate for each country but of course in reality exchange rates would rise and fall daily. We made sure we took our foreign notes to Thomas Cook on a 'good' day! Taking foreign banknotes gave us quite a headache as there were no calculators, so scrap paper and some rapid maths were called for. An example might be, "One and a half singles to Bradford please and I only have Australian currency…." With the Aussie pound then worth perhaps 15s 5d the brain was taxed to the hilt!

One of the perks of the job was seeing and meeting celebrities, most then travelling by sea. I remember Sir Anthony Eden arriving and looking very sick. Some celebrities were difficult to pick out in the crowd but there was no doubt about Tommy Steele with his boyish grin and sparkling white teeth. Some also had fan clubs and these would charter a train to meet people like Bill Haley or Liberace. I thus got my first glimpse of mass hysteria.

But let us get back to ticket issuing. As I said every boat was different and a liner called the *Homeric*, regularly brought in passengers who had bought thrift coupons abroad. Each coupon, about 1cm square, was valued at either 6d or 2/6. We, of course, took full pages of coupons and no change was given, so, again, the mental arithmetic kicked in 'eight half crowns to a pound….', then make up the rest with odd coupons.

In the 1950s, immigrants from the West Indies were arriving in the country in large numbers and in these cases they all had to purchase tickets. This is the only time I can ever remember boat trains going direct to destinations other than London as Midlands' destinations were also involved. I also recall one particularly busy Saturday when Waterloo was simply too busy to accept much in the way of boat traffic and instead some services were diverted to Victoria.

When those arriving from the Caribbean purchased tickets they might use their own local bank notes, but strangely this was usually accompanied by our coins. Much of this was old silver - and I mean old. It was also a very

Ticket issuing from a portable ticket office. Notwithstanding the number of potential travellers, security was minimal.

slow process as they were understandably cautious, but we were also slow as we could not believe what we were seeing. I still have a William IV shilling which I exchanged from the till. How I wish I could have afforded to buy out more old silver, it would have been worth a fortune now.

We were also never bored when in the Docks. There might be troopships arriving, again almost all going on boat trains, but the men would have travel warrants so we took no money. We had a tray of forces' duty tickets; to London, yes, but also to other destinations with military association, e.g. Catterick, Aldershot: and although most were individual, we had a few where we would use a paper ticket, as it might be for a service family or perhaps an officer and 15 other ranks travelling together.

We could enquire in advance which regiments were on board and thus take tickets to appropriate destinations - once on board there was no turning back! get some idea of the likely work ahead by asking the first ones in the queue if a whole regiment was coming back then. These would include tickets for some local stations applicable to the regiment's home base - but we would dread the Welsh regiments with the obvious spelling problems. Upon the return to the office all these had been

sorted, although this might take several days as opposed to other ships when a cash balance had to be struck as soon as possible.

The last types of 'passenger' to talk about were the crews themselves. In these cases we went on board the ship. Crew members were not allowed on boat trains, so again, we had another set of tickets, 'Mercantile Marine on leave', at 5/7th of station fare, (not boat train fares) and our printed destinations were, for example, Hull, Liverpool, Grimsby, etc. If it was a small ship like a banana boat, there would only be a handful of tickets to issue; but if, for instance, the *Queen Mary* was paying off, this would be an enormous exercise and, of course, lots of money was taken but some were entitled to free tickets and this meant ordinary single tickets given in exchange for a warrant.

Southampton was never dull at that time!

(A previous article by Tony Carter: 'Station Master - Steyning' appeared in SW19. More of Tony's memories will also feature in SW in the future. Tony is also author of the book 'To the Railway Born: Reminiscences of Station Life, 1934 - 1992' published by Silver Link.)

US Army Transportation Corps No 4326 shunting in Southampton Docks with a Southern Railway crew, April 1947. This engine had been built in 1943 and was purchased by the SR in May 1946. It was allocated SR No 74 but this was never carried and instead it went straight into BR livery as No 30074.

CICESTRIAN CAMEOS

One time resident, *Jeffery Grayer,* recalls the surprising variety of motive power through the cathedral city of Chichester, county town of West Sussex, situated as it was deep in the heart of *"Southern Electric"* territory.

34098 "Templecombe" in original condition calls at Chichester with the through train from Brighton to Plymouth. The fireman takes the opportunity of the stop to rake some coal forward in the tender. This Pacific was allocated to Brighton from March 1959 – November 1960 thus dating this shot to that period, the locomotive being rebuilt in Jan/Feb 1961 and lasting until the end of SR steam in July 1967.

Living in Chichester during the 1960s, one was accustomed to a largely unrelieved diet of Southern Region electric multiple units for much of the day. However there were three scheduled appearances of steam on passenger workings in the form of through trains from Brighton to the West. These comprised the : -

    09:40   Brighton – Bournemouth

    11:00   Brighton – Cardiff

    11:30   Brighton – Plymouth

plus of course their respective return workings.

The Bournemouth service was withdrawn in the winter of 1961/2 thereafter running during the summer on Sundays only until it was permanently withdrawn from September 1964. The Cardiff service went in 1963.

Without doubt the most prestigious of these through trains was the Plymouth service as it had a Buffet Car throughout and, with a section from Portsmouth being added at Fareham, the combined train was often loaded to 11 coaches or more and sported carriage-boards proclaiming **"BRIGHTON – PORTSMOUTH – SOUTHAMPTON – EXETER & PLYMOUTH"**. On summer Saturdays, such was the demand, that a separate train from Portsmouth – Plymouth was provided for a time. This was also a particularly useful service for naval personnel based at the

Left - The view from the Westgate Fields footbridge situated to the west of the station reveals the well stocked goods yard, an E5xxx locomotive and a passing semi-fast service from Brighton to Portsmouth & Southsea formed of 2-BIL stock.

Opposite bottom - In 1967 Flying Scotsman paid a visit to south coast metals when it headed a railtour on 17 September 1966 achieving speeds in the 80's on its run through Sussex. It is seen here powering through the station on its return journey to London.

two great dockyards. There was generally an engine change at Salisbury where the locomotive from Brighton gave way to a Salisbury-based one which worked through to Exeter or Plymouth. This service was particularly attractive to enthusiasts not only for the chance to ride behind steam in one of Bulleid's comfortable coaches but because it provided one of the rare chances to travel to Salisbury without the tiresome necessity of going into Fratton and out again having changed into the 'delights' of a Hampshire DEMU for the onward journey. Added to these attractions was the chance to sample the Buffet Car even if the constraints of pocket money meant one had to be content merely with morning coffee served by white coated stewards from silver coffee pots into real china!

U1 Class 31890 takes water with the through train from Brighton to Plymouth. The bay platform to the right housed local services from Chichester – Portsmouth serving all stations and halts. The bay to the left once saw the departure of Midhurst trains until closure to passengers in 1935. The use of a U1 on such a prestige service was unusual and indeed on 19 November 1960 nothing better than No 31890 could be found by Brighton shed staff to power this service with the Mogul struggling as far as Yeovil Junction where it was replaced. This shot was taken prior to rebuilding of the old station, which by the early 1960s had become very decrepit, and was replaced with state of the art modern image buildings.

Bulleid Pacifics invariably worked these prestige services until the mid '60s but despite the fact that they were based at Brighton for a number of years, the majority having been built at the Works there, it was often said that the staff there never really mastered the intricacies of these complex machines, and other types such as Maunsell Moguls, Schools and Standard classes regularly deputised. My journey home from school invariably involved a detour via the railway station where steam could be expected at 16:30 from Plymouth. As often as not the locomotive would be one of a quartet of Bulleids which became rather monotonous to us enthusiasts, invariably *"Padstow", "Bideford", "Lynton"* or *"Fighter Pilot"*. What would one give for such predictability today !

Bulleid Pacifics allocated to Brighton (75A) in the 1960s		
34008	*Padstow*	Oct 58 - Sep 62
34012	*Launceston*	Jul 62 - Sep 63
34013	*Okehampton*	Jul 62 - Sep 63
34014	*Budleigh Salterton*	Jul 62 – Sep 63
34019	*Bideford*	Oct 58 – Sep 63
34027	*Taw Valley*	May 61 - Sep 63
34038	*Lynton*	Nov 60 - Nov 61
34055	*Fighter Pilot*	Mar 60 - Jun 63
34057	*Biggin Hill*	Nov 60 - Sep 63
34063	*229 Squadron*	May 63 - Sep 63
34088	*213 Squadron*	Jun 63 - Jul 63
34089	*602 Squadron*	Nov 62 - Sep 63
34097	*Holsworthy*	Mar 59 - Nov 60
34098	*Templecombe*	Mar 59 -Nov 60
34099	*Lynmouth*	Mar 59 - Mar 60
34100	*Appledore*	Nov 62 - Sep 63
34101	*Hartland*	Jul 62 - Jun 63

Being the changeover point from South Western to Central Division motive power, a considerable variety of goods locomotives were to be seen, some favourites being the regular appearance of members of the King Arthur class from Eastleigh on the goods which arrived at 8 o'clock in the evening. In the winter, with dark evenings, it was often impossible to see the loco's number so a call to the crew often elicited the requisite information! S15s, Maunsell moguls and Standards also performed on freight services, handing over to K Class Moguls for their journey eastwards. Some very unusual locomotives turned up from time to time, presumably being spare at Eastleigh, and on one occasion in 1964, 21 September to be exact, Ivatt 2-6-0 No 43066 from 40E Colwick depot arrived, probably the first of its class to touch Sussex metals. Black 5 No 45379 was also another probable first for this type when on 15 April 1964 it was used for a Chichester – Bournville excursion, the locomotive having worked the empty stock from Willesden to Brighton a couple of days previously.

Other notable visitors were *"The Great Marquess"* in 1966 and *"Flying Scotsman"* in 1967 both on railtours. With the closure of Brighton shed in 1964, electric locomotives of E5xxx type and from the trio 20001-3 were more frequently seen on eastbound freight services together with Crompton diesels. Shunters of Class 08 were used to shunt the yard and to trip up to Lavant in the sugar beet season. Members of Maunsell's SR design of diesel shunter, Nos 15201-3, were also noted on occasion until their withdrawal in 1964. all in all, a surprisingly eclectic mix of motive power for a location deep in Southern Electric territory.

Left - *No 34020 "Seaton" is captured departing from Chichester with a through service from Brighton. Note the water cranes on the left often used by goods locomotives and those making use of the turning triangle.*

Below - *No 34019 "Bideford" (a long-time Brighton depot stalwart of the through trains to the West of England) has just left the station eastbound and, having crossed the level crossing, passes a gasholder on the left and the wall of the Southdown Bus Station the latter conveniently located adjacent to the station on the right.*

Opposite top - *Having failed, in service, Standard Class 5 No 73043 is parked out of use on one of the goods yard sidings, the "pep pipe" hanging forlornly from the cab window.*

Opposite bottom - *Q1 No C15, latterly No 33015, stands in Chichester Yard with a mixed freight in 1947 shortly before nationalisation. A C2X lurks in the background. (Rail Photoprints)*

CHICHESTER - YESTERYEAR

Opposite top- Class E5 No 2592 ambles through Chichester with a short trip freight in 1947. (Rail Photoprints)

Opposite bottom - Class K No 2344 struggles away from Chichester with a Brighton-bound freight in 1949, still sporting its pre nationalisation number. (Rail Photoprints)

Right - C2X 32549 poses in the yard on 9 April 1955. (Rail Photoprints)

On 20 September 1952, H15 No 30331 is seen having just turned on the triangle, one arm of which can be seen to the left in this view. Note the small stage to the right, filled with clinker, and the brace of water columns to be seen behind an unidentified tank locomotive. (Rail Photoprints)

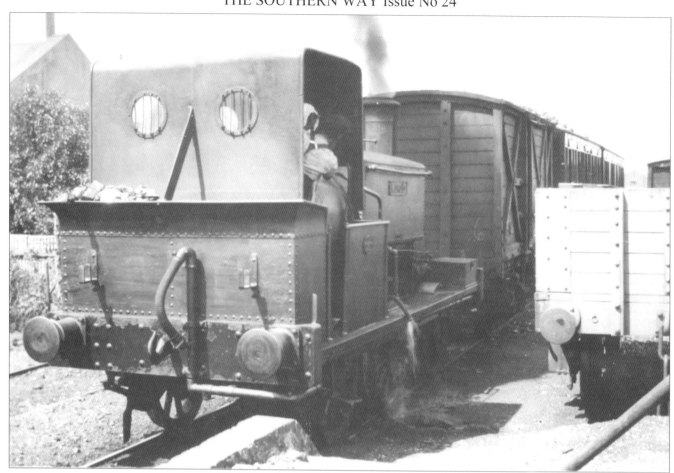

No visit to Chichester and its environs would be complete without reference to the Selsey Tram, or to be more precise 'The Hundred of Manhood and Selsey Tramway'. (See also issue No 5 of 'SW'.)

In the view **top left** is 'Morous', originally purchased as 'used'* in 1910 by Col Stephens for use on his Shropshire & Montgomery system and later transferred south in 1924. It would be interesting to know how engines were moved between the various Col Stephens lines, on their own wheels or as part of a load, if the latter no doubt having various fittings removed to comply with respective loading gauge requirements. We know that after it arrived the engine was repainted but this new paint weathered away so that by the time of closure it displayed the liveries of both lines. (* the engine had been built by Manning Wardle in 1866 and so was already 44 years old when acquired by the Colonel.)

Opposite bottom - 'Selsey; a 2-4-2T by Peckett in 1897 and the only new steam engine bought for the railway. When just 11 years-old this engine was found to require a new firebox, although presumably the replacement was of good quality as there is no reference to further replacement for the remainder of its life. It is seen here in charge of a mixed train crossing Pagham Harbour.

Above - The same engine, this time at Chichester heading away towards Selsey. With the main line Southern railway system in the background, also to be seen is a private owner wagon lettered 'Arnall', a local merchant.

Terry Cole's Rolling Stock File No. 24
LSWR 'Gate' Stock

As a boy in the 1950s I lived by the railway line in Worthing and would see the empty stock transfer trains between Lancing and Micheldever or Eastleigh usually hauled by a 'K' or 'H2'. Mostly the stock on these trains is now but a hazy memory, apart from one type of coach – one which didn't have doors but had gates! So it was that I encountered the last examples of ex-LSWR 'Gate' stock, arguably the most distinctive of all Southern stock and once seen was never forgotten.

The Gate stock had its origins in the steam railmotors built in the early years of this century and when these proved unsatisfactory many of the passenger sections were rebuilt into locomotive-hauled coaches but still retaining their original entry gates. In 1906 six new 48ft long 'vestibule cars', as they were called, were built. These had gates in the 'middle' of each coach and were formed into three two-coach push-pull sets comprising a Driving Brake 3rd and a Trailer 3rd, later becoming SR sets 367 – 9.

Opposite - Here we see S2622S the Driving saloon brake 3rd of set 373 [originally SR Diagram 414, 129 as all third] at Plymouth Friary on 21 August 1956. The former 1st class saloon was nearest to the brake to the left of the gate entrance.

Above - Next to S2622S is S738S a trailer 3rd and the other half of set 373. This was to SR Diagram 27. The vehicles had a gangway connection between them. Set 373 lasted until 1960 and was selected for preservation on the Bluebell Railway but it suffered storm damage that autumn and was scrapped.

These were withdrawn c1939/40. Further stock was built in 1909, this time 56 ft. long (SR sets Nos 370/1). Another three two coach push-pull sets of 56ft stock were ordered in1913 comprising a Driving brake composite and a Trailer 3rd. It is these coaches which are the subject of this 'File'. They became sets Nos 372-4 and were downgraded to all-third in 1929. Most prominent for the passenger and the observer were the elaborate wrought iron gates which gave access to the coach. Inside the trailer coach were two saloons, one either side of the gate. The smaller had two windows worth of longitudinal seating and a bay of the usual open coach seating, the larger having the same longitudinal seats plus four bays of open seating. The driving coach had a large 3rd class saloon with conventional open seating and a first class saloon with longitudinal bench seating.

Although associated with the Plymouth area all their lives, Gate stock could at various times be found on a number of minor LSWR branches, including Callington, Lee-on-the-Solent, Bordon etc. Set No 372 was split in the 1920s with the brake composite allocated to the Bishops Waltham line until its closure in 1933. The set was then reformed but now as set number 363, which identification it retained until withdrawn in November 1958.

This is Trailer 3rd S739S of set 374 at Plymouth Friary in August 1954. Driving Saloon Brake S2624S is behind. The set number is painted (additionally) on the non-driving end of the set, an unusual feature often found on Gate sets. This set was withdrawn in the autumn of 1956.

All photos David Wigley

Bob Winkworth has been in touch to ask if anyone can identify what this tender was used for - recorded at Eastleigh, would you believe, on 1 April 1967! So far we have come up with a water carrier as part of a weed-killing train but any further thoughts would be appreciated.

And to prove that we are not totally besotted with Southern steam and electric topics, this image recently arrived with us but with no details as to location. We are guessing a test run with a new D65xx, any thoughts…?

Mr Bulleid's rebuilds

We are delighted to present a small selection of colour images from the camera of Roger Thornton, who was recording the scene on the 'racing' section of the former South Western main line between Basingstoke and Farnborough between 1958 and 1966.

Left is No 34056 'Croydon' London-bound, recorded in Winchfield Cutting amidst the haze of a summer's day, 20 August 1966. The view is impossible to replicate today, not just for the engine and stock but mainly due to the presence of a concrete flyover taking the M3 motorway over the railway at this point.

Above - No 35022 'Holland America Line' at speed with the Up 'Royal Wessex' in 1958. The BR Mk1 stock used for this train will be noted. 'The Royal Wessex' was considered by many crews to be amongst the hardest workings on the South Western division, partly because of its weight but also due to the stops made with little compromise as regards the timings.

Colour images - Roger Thornton / Noodle Books collection.

This page - For comparison sake, passing under one of the low-pressure pneumatic signal gantries so typical of this section of line. No 34015 'Exmouth' is near Fleet with the 17.30 down from Waterloo on an unreported date.

Opposite top - No 35022 again, although perhaps not quite so clean as in 1958. This time the location is recorded, Pirbright, and the date July 1965.

Opposite bottom - No 34034 'Honiton' at Farnborough on 9 September 1961 with an Air Show special.

SOUTHERN INFRASTRUTURE 1922 - 1934
Stations / Signalling / Trackwork
Photographs from the E. Wallis collection

In compiling 'Southern Way' it has been a privilege to view some remarkable material. Often negotiations have been successful in securing its use, infrequently not, but it has still been a pleasure and privilege.

Every so often though something really remarkable come along, and this has been the case with the Wallis archive. As many will be aware, what we hope will be just the first book from this collection will be published by us around the time this issue of 'SW' is released. I can do no more than that: provide a photographic taster with a few pages from the actual book and also introduce the collection with the introduction used within the actual book.

"I had known of the existence of the Wallis collection for many years, a few having 'escaped' in the past, principally in the 1980s which appeared in various albums produced by Middleton Press. (More recently the odd one has appeared in publications produced by the Signalling Record Society and also in 'Southern Way'.) Having had my own appetite whetted, I had always wondered what else might be 'lurking' and it was thus a privilege to meet David Wallis in 2012 and arrange a schedule to produce not only what is a photographic tribute to the work of his late father Edward Wallis, but at the same time a tribute to the Southern Railway.

"Edward Wallis may not have been alone in having

access to the lineside in the period in question (although he did get to some places others may not have done), but he was probably unique in recording the infrastructure of the Southern Railway - meaning primarily the signalling - at that time.

"From the perspective of a researcher, being passed what turned out to be tray after tray of glass plates was like being a child in the proverbial sweet shop. There were perhaps 250 negatives in each tray, each contained within a paper packet, written thereon a brief description, mostly even with a date appended. Reading the words immediately led me to wonder what joy might be contained therein and which in many cases had lain unseen by human eyes for, in some cases, decades. I was rarely disappointed.

"Whilst this was going on, David Wallis appeared sometimes even surprised at my joyous reaction and whilst understandably he may not have been able to recount the exact reference number and tray position for each, he displayed a remarkable memory for knowing if a view of a specific location existed in the collection.

"In all there are in the order of 1,500 glass plates,

SOUTHERN INFRASTRUCTURE
1922-1938 | STATIONS/SIGNALLING/TRACKWORK
Photographs from the E Wallis Collection

mostly contemporary with the late E Wallis, but some were earlier still, clearly copies and which had been annotated as such. Thus we have views going back to the turn of the 20th century and in some cases beforehand, it is only appropriate if these fit into our journey that they should be included.

"In what will quickly be seen as a remarkable and probably unique collection of contemporary images, two thoughts will immediately come to mind. The first, an assumption that every location on the Southern was photographed - if only it were thus - and that because they are glass negatives then the quality will be perfect in every case. Again, if only it were so.

"E Wallis recorded the images sometimes whilst he was at work as a signal engineer, taking his camera and plates with him, and other times possibly on a day-off or whilst travelling on holiday, hence there also exists a limited number of signalling views away from the Southern. Access and inconvenient train timing also meant some routes and locations have been totally ignored whilst others were clearly favourites and revisited on a number of occasions.

"It must also be recalled that using and taking an image with a plate camera from the top of a tall signal post swaying gracefully in the breeze (even if no wind was apparent at ground level) called for a steady nerve and a steady hand. Consequently it must be said far from all were a 100% success, whilst lighting conditions, hardly an issue with today's digital technology, meant a number are unfortunately simply too dark to be included. In this he was hardly alone. The days of 'wet film technology' and which most readers will remember, were punctuated with as many failures as there were successes. What appeared perfectly

We move south now to Purley and where on 9 May 1929 the camera was pointed at three examples of the signalling in the area. **Opposite page** is the Purley North Signal Box up starting signal and with its lower arm repeated. The mixture of overhead electric and third-rail will also be noted.

Above left - Purley North Signal Box down inner home (main) group. The shunt signal is shown in what was reported to be its normal 'off' position.

Above right - Purley, 'Up Tatterham Corner Home Signal Group', albeit consisting of just a single post with two arms. The Calling On arm is slightly unusual being painted with just one red stripe. It is also of interest in that it is nearly full length. The origins of this arm are clearly SECR, which company arranged their CO arms with a hollow diamond on the arm. Both were painted red. It is likely this arm has been up graded quickly with the diamond replaced with the standard C and some white paint slapped on to cover the red but which then only left one red stripe! Purley was one of those locations where the meeting of what was originally LBSCR and SECR metals meant the origins of the actual signalling was apt to be confusing.

51

fine to the human eye through the viewfinder could be an abject disappointment when processed in the darkroom or returned from the chemist.

"But when it worked, it worked superbly, as witness the examples within these pages. I do hope you both appreciate and enjoy what follows, it has certainly been a privilege to have been allowed access to the collection. To this end I must therefore record my grateful thanks to David Wallis and the Wallis family for their trust and co-operation in this venture.

"Should the reader feel their appetite for this type of material has perhaps not quite been sated, all I can say is that there is certainly enough for a further album."

Kevin Robertson
(Sorry to be cruel but if you do not recognise all the locations you will have to buy the book!)

The junction at Christchurch after simplification of the layout in August 1928. From this time until 1937, a single lead was provided on to the Ringwood line with a new trailing crossover between the up and down main lines behind the camera.

Copyhold (Junction) signal box, undated but certainly later than the two track views as electrification has taken place in the interim. Notice below the name the number '2243' painted on to the boarding. Was this a structure identification number? It is certainly something that appears to have been used by the LBSCR but was evidently not copied by the Southern.

Copyhold Up Home Signal with a blind top arm - the top arm will be seen to be minus a spectacle. 3 March 1923.

Southerham Junction was the point of divergence for the line to Newhaven and Seaford from the coastal route to St Leonards. A signal box of sorts was reported here as early as 1856 with the present structure to a Saxby & Farmer design provided in 1874. 21 levers were provided with the box also controlling access to a chalk quarry on the down of the line. 3 May 1924.

SOME GEMS FROM A WORKING TIMETABLE

Jeremy Clarke

I find 'Remaindered' books a source of fascination. Though it is easy to see why some volumes sit for years gathering dust on a retailer's shelves - and I wonder how, in that light, any publisher could have been so optimistic as to consider issuing them - for others to do so is a mystery. Forty-odd years ago I picked up one such book in just such a shop close to South Kensington underground station. Yet I find it so interesting and informative, indeed quirky in places, I still do not understand why it found its way there. I must have made the purchase about the time decimal currency superseded good old pounds, shillings and pence because the price on the flyleaf is quoted as '55s, £2.75'. Both, however, have been crossed through with a single swift sweep of a pen - a proper ink one too, no Biro this! - and '25/-' writ large and defiantly in their place.

The book is a facsimile copy of the London & South Western Railway Working Timetables for the summer of 1909 and makes fascinating reading. The book itself, published by Ian Allan, appears to be at least the seventh in a series though with no publishing date that I can find. It is about A5 in size and despite the very small typeface the printed matter is about 1¼" thick. Perhaps as a sign of the importance the Superintendent of the Line, Henry Holmes, attached to this prestige document the opening pages of each section use no fewer than nine different fonts.

The first surprise was to find that the 'Main Line' is not, as might be expected, Waterloo-Salisbury-Exeter but Waterloo to Southampton. Surprise was tempered at a second glance when it became clear the book is divided into the three Districts of the Railway as they were then, Main Line and Central District, Metropolitan District, and

L12 4-4-0 No 427 with a West of England express. The presence of the 3rd rail indicates the location as somewhere fairly close to the London area. Note the locomotive coupling is of the standard 3-link type.

Western District and the Salisbury & Yeovil Line. Another quick run-through posed another question: why were the Central and Metropolitan Districts segregated when the former would now be considered without doubt part of the Metropolitan area? After a little rumination the answer was quite clear, that many parts of present-day London were then still quite separate from the capital, the furthest ones probably not yet even considered as outer-suburbia.

The particular reference to the Salisbury & Yeovil is interesting for although the South Western had purchased the company in 1878, it still is seemingly considered as a separate concern thirty years later. The LSWR had been authorised to build this line in 1848, but had never got around to it because of squabbling among shareholders and between them and the Board. The Company watched with rather smug interest as an independent concern received sanction to construct it instead, increasingly confident the S&Y, which had much trouble raising capital, would subside into bankruptcy resulting in the South Western being able to purchase it at a knockdown price. In time all found themselves guilty of a serious error of judgement for the impecunious concern got to Gillingham in May 1859 and completed its line to Yeovil on 1st June 1860, six weeks before the South Western opened from Yeovil through to Exeter. The Salisbury & Yeovil proved to be a real money-spinner, paying a dividend of 12½% by 1877. When the South Western came to purchase it the next year, having worked the line from the beginning, it had to hand over no less than £260 of its own Stock for each nominal £100 of S&YR shares.

Returning to the book, it is very likely the various divisions were despatched to the Districts to which they refer and only senior officers in the Running Departments would have had a full copy. Rather than examine each of these in turn, this article will concentrate on the first, the Main Line and Central Districts, simply because being the largest it probably has the greatest variety of workings.

What follows the title page is enlightening. After the index there are two pages that reflect quite starkly the difference between a working railway a century ago and that of today. Meticulous instructions are given for supplying every signalbox, no matter how close to or how remote from a station, with coal and stores. The staff at Wimbledon, for example, are required to fill sacks with coal for Wimbledon Yard and Wimbledon West signalboxes and have them 'sent down by shunting engine as required'. Byfleet Junction and Addlestone Junction boxes have their stores supplied by Weybridge station, the Weybridge shunting loco being used to transport them, the "Station Inspector or Head Porter to travel on the engine".

Next come several pages listing the working of Mixed Trains under the Regulation of Railways Act 1889, then a number of specific rules to do with the speed of trains, two pages of permanent speed restrictions, a catalogue of locomotives prohibited from running on certain lines, speed restrictions issued by the other companies over whose lines LSWR trains travel and then no fewer than twenty-eight pages of close type listing every train alteration since the last issue, all those affecting this one District.

Then we actually get to the timetables. One immediate difference is that trains are consecutively numbered in both up and down directions whereas common practice for years has been to allocate odd numbers to down trains and even numbers to up ones. The second difference is, of course, that the 24-hour clock is not used, so every column is headed 'am' or pm' as appropriate. Distances are marked in miles and chains from Waterloo, the first table, the Main Line, having two sets of mileages because at that time trains still went to Winchester and Southampton via the Mid-Hants line, a distance, be it remarked, 57 chains less than via Basingstoke.

This table also displays some other peculiarities. For example, it includes the New Malden (then Coombe & Malden) to Teddington line and the Hampton Court branch as well as the Farnham and Alton line and its continuation to Winchester. But the line to Epsom, the Guildford New Line, Weybridge-Virginia Water via Chertsey and, perhaps most astonishingly, the Portsmouth Direct are all omitted though references are made to all four in the headings of individual services. Down train No 21 for example, the 1.40am Portsmouth Goods *(Not Mondays),* passes Hampton Court Junction at 2.12 with the note following that it travels the 'Claygate and Guildford Line'. Similarly No 60, the 4.50am 'Pass Virginia Water' arrives at Weybridge at 5.41 and departs at 5.55 though those times are both heavily underlined which would normally imply in more recent editions that the train terminates.

Some entries are for types of trains that simply do not exist on today's railways. Examples are represented by the simultaneous departures from Waterloo at 3.0am of No 30, a newspaper train to Portsmouth via Eastleigh, a routing that continued right up to and beyond the end of steam, and No 31, a milk churn train to Yeovil, another traffic now lost entirely to the railways. The former incidentally was already three minutes ahead of the latter by Queen's Road. Then Nos 96 and 97 down are both noted as *'Cattle Wednesdays only when required',* the former from Basingstoke to Winchester, the latter between Alresford and Southampton. Those entries highlight a practice common for years, that paths had to be found among the regular services for trains that ran only on certain days of the week or when traffic offering required them to be run. As will be shown shortly, trains on the Main Line had to be scheduled to leave room for the prestige Boat Trains to Southampton Docks, a major source of income at that time and indeed for years to come.

The inevitable improvement in speed in a century is also noteworthy. For example, No 145, 'Pass Roundabout', leaves Waterloo at 8.25am, arriving at Teddington via Kingston at 9.17, a journey of 52 minutes: today it takes nineteen minutes less though whether the electric South West Trains class 455 with its hard,

We now move to the eastern end of Salisbury station with a pair of Adams 4-4-0s. The ornate livery complete with the LSWR crest on the leading splasher and polished brasswork would have made a stunning sight.

unyielding if ergonomic seats can match the stuffed comfort of even 3rd class in steam-hauled South Western suburban stock is debatable.

Other apparent anomalies show in services numbered 166/7/8 as all leave Waterloo at 9.20am. It is only as one progresses down the columns that things become clearer. No 166 is marked as 'Pass to Bournemouth' and makes its first call at Surbiton at 9.40, departing two minutes later for Woking Junction where it arrives at 9.59. No 167 is 'Pass to Fareham' and at first glance non-stop to Woking where it arrives at the same time as No 166. However, it departs three minutes after that one from which, clearly, it has been detached. It then proceeds as a 'stopper', passing Butts Junction at 11.13, and then disappears altogether until reappearing over 100 pages later in the Meon Valley timetable, a route that has long vanished from railway maps. One riddle presented here is that this train makes its first call after Woking at North Camp. A quick consultation with Dendy Marshall shows that that LSWR station was renamed Ash Vale in 1924 to make a clear differentiation with the station on the SER line and Camberley.

Meanwhile No 166 has continued on its merry way with calls at Basingstoke, Winchester and Eastleigh at which point No 168 appears to have travelled non-stop but arrived at the same time. The giveaway is the same as

before, No 166, having detached No 168 there, departing five minutes ahead of it. Beyond the fact that No 168 is 'Pass', there is no indication of its ultimate destination though it turns out, as the train calls at Northam, to be the Southampton station later suffixed 'Terminus'. To find the fate of no 166 it is necessary to go forward no fewer than 125 pages to the timetable covering the routes to Bournemouth and Weymouth. There we find that the train has called at Southampton West (later Central) between 11.38 and 11.42 before running non-stop to Brockenhurst from where it becomes an all-stations stopper to Bournemouth West via Sway, arriving at 1.24pm. But the letter 'B' at the head of the column shows there is footnote. It reads, "Runs on Local Line from Woking East and Through Line from Woking Junction to Basingstoke East, except when 9.28am Boat Train runs, when it will run on Local Line Marsh Lane Box to Woking and follow Boat Train at latter point, and when 9.45am Boat Train runs it will run on Local Line from Basingstoke East and follow the Boat Train from Worting Box". There is also a comment that the call at Surbiton is to pick up only. The 9.28 Boat Train runs *'When Required'*, the 9.45 only on Wednesdays, but again *'When Required'*. I wonder if a signalman ever got it wrong!

On that same page is another throwback to routes impossible to travel nowadays. No 176 down is headed

At least four decades later and No 30862 'Lord Collingwood' is recorded at Fleet on a down boat train for Southampton.

E C Griffiths

'Windsor to Guildford' which, from the fact it does not call at Staines [Junction], made use of the long-gone north to west curve there. However, there are only three timings in the column, the passing time at Byfleet Junction, and arrival and departure times at Byfleet and at Woking. This train only otherwise appears in a later table that covers the group of 'Windsor Lines' which surprisingly included Neasden, Brent and Willesden via Acton Wells for freight workings. Despite a fairly careful search the onward few miles of the Windsor train between Woking and Guildford have so far eluded me.

So, having taken no fewer than 110 pages to dispose of the Main Line and its three specified offshoots one might have expected the next table would have shown at least a continuation beyond Basingstoke towards Salisbury or one or other of the lines branching off the Main Line that do not appear in that table. Not a bit of it! Next comes one page detailing the trains on the DN&S line despite the fact these have already appeared in the previous timetable. However, this one includes timings at Winchester 'Didcot Line' station (Chesil) but nothing north of there because that is GWR territory. As the Winchester to Shawford Junction section is single track the train identification in the column headings specify the issue of Staff or Ticket to permit the driver entry to it. Though this never was a particularly busy line there is only one train each way on Sunday and that worked throughout by the Great Western.

Next is a summary of trains between Eastleigh and Southampton. There are some puzzling anomalies here too.

For example, why does the London-Royal Pier service arriving at Southampton at 7.52am show in both tables, but the train from Portsmouth that joins the main line at St Denys, due at Southampton at 8.25am, only appears in the Summary? The following goods from Fratton is treated likewise. Curious.

Further perusal leads one to the conclusion that tables appear almost in the order in which the lines to which they refer are situated. The further west one travels, each specific tentacle of those lines is considered in turn irrespective of their relative importance. No greater contrast with the busy Eastleigh-Southampton section could be made than by the next three tables, Bentley and Bordon Light, Basingstoke and Alton Light (of 'The Wrecker' and 'Oh! Mr Porter' fame) and Meon Valley, suffixed Alton and Fareham Line. Thereafter another chunk of main line, Basingstoke-Salisbury, breaks up the continuing series of byways.

Shown here is the sequence of trains that later, in part anyway, caused a further widening of the irreparable rift between Henry Holmes and Herbert Walker. The longstanding mid-morning Plymouth Express, leaving at 10.45, is followed at 11.10am by the Torrington train, both fast to Salisbury in 91 and 94 minutes respectively. However, daily from the 10th July to 29th September, a North Cornwall Express is scheduled to leave between these two at 11.0am. That also is non-stop to Salisbury in 94 minutes though all three trains change engines at Sarum for which the 10.45 and 11.0 o'clock are both allowed five minutes. But that means the third of the three comes into Salisbury right on the heels of the second. Records indicate that the choice of engine for these trains appeared to be quite arbitrary and a Drummond 'double-single' leaving Waterloo on the 10.45 was shown often to have some difficulty keeping the 91-minute schedule with any load exceeding 200 tons. Thus even the thirteen minutes between the departure of the first of the trio and the arrival of the second did not always prove adequate, though engine changing at Salisbury was renowned for its swiftness. The five minutes between departure of the second train from Salisbury and the timely arrival of the third could be even more problematic, especially if the former were headed by a double-single! One wonders how things worked out when, up to the end of the 19th century, all three ran regularly but left Waterloo at ten-minute intervals, 10.50, 11.0 and 11.10, the last of the trio being booked to Salisbury in the fastest time.

Also in this table is a reminder that sources of coal were wholly absent from the South Western system. A train of Loco Coal Empties departs from Nine Elms at 7.15am: its progress is sluggish to say the least. Two hours and twenty-three minutes are spent reaching Basingstoke where it sits down for half-an-hour to let the crew have their mid-morning 'snap' while the 8.50am Waterloo-Plymouth train passes. Fifty minutes are taken thereafter to Andover Junction for a 1½-hour lunch break and then a slow tailing of the 11.10 Waterloo-Torrington passenger train for the bare 6½ miles to Grateley. Here another one-hour stop is scheduled and another Waterloo summer departure, at 11.15am for Exeter, passes. Salisbury is finally reached at 2.15pm, seven hours after setting off from London.

Clearly the trip is more than simply running the train and hanging about at some intermediate stations. Additional empties may have been picked up from the shed at Basingstoke for example, perhaps elsewhere also though no pick-up points are stipulated. No doubt the train will have been periodically examined for hot boxes and perhaps

the brakes pinned down on a few of vehicles for the 10-mile downhill run to Salisbury. There is no departure time shown there so it is fair to assume the train is handed over to the GWR for forwarding via Westbury. Drummond's monstrous and monumentally unsuccessful 'F13' class "Express" (?) 4-6-0s may well have taken a hand in such a working. Incidentally, a footnote regarding this train indicates it will call on Wednesdays at stations west of Woking to pick up any cattle traffic for Basingstoke market. Perhaps this puts into a degree of perspective the generous running time permitted and the half-hour scheduled at the latter place. However, it also calls at Porton on Mondays if there is any Road Box traffic to be dealt with; and at Amesbury Junction when required to put off stores. So then, not always purely a train of loco-coal empties as implied after all.

Amongst the longer distance traffic in this table is the spasmodic heading 'Fullerton Motor 1st and 3rd classes only'. The main line junction for these trains is Whitchurch and after the call at Hurstbourne they vanish to re-appear in the following table on another long-gone line that once went through to Romsey via Stockbridge, following the picturesque valley of the River Test. Fullerton, the third station down this route, was the terminus for the 'Motors' and the junction for a line from Andover considered the more important of the two and therefore bagging the 'through' services to Southampton. But to find those one has to search forward again, sixty-odd pages this time.

Services between Salisbury or Andover and the military camp at Bulford merit a separate table. There are two return goods workings daily, one each from the two mainline stations, while Salisbury despatches seven passenger trains and receives eight: two run in each direction to/from Andover. Sunday sees one morning down train from the two main line stations but no up workings at all except a single empty stock train to Salisbury. That alone might be thought to have caused problems for soldiers with a weekend pass although the answer here is simple, at

Branch line time. A military special at Amesbury probably not long after the branch line had opened. The two engines coupled tender to tender is perhaps slightly unusual unless this is an amalgam of two trains which had arrived from different directions.

The Ringwood motor posed alongside the original station at Christchurch although superseded by a resited station consequent upon the opening of the direct line to Bournemouth via Sway. LSWR 'Gate' stock is in use coupled to one of Mr Drummond's two diminutive S14 0-4-0T engines. (Deemed to be of limited use, both machines of the S14 type were sold by Drummond's successor Robert Urie to the Ministry of Munitions in May 1917.)

that time there was no such thing as a week-end pass!

Red Post Junction, west of Andover was, of course, the point at which another independent, the Midland & South Western Junction Railway, the great little 'Tiddley Dyke', joined the South Western. It worked half-a-dozen trains, passenger and freight, each way to/from Southampton, about a quarter of the total services. On Sundays the MSWJ ran a goods train to and from Romsey but only a single morning passenger departure from Southampton, at 8.53, the stock being provided by a Saturdays only late-evening working.

After the Fullerton line timetable come those of the Salisbury & Dorset – another lost route, to Bournemouth West via Fordingbridge and Wimborne – and the very much alive one between Eastleigh and Weymouth. The latter includes the Lymington and Swanage branches and 'Castleman's Corkscrew' via Ringwood and Wimborne, as well as the cut-off from that route through Hurn and the later and surviving main line via Sway. Tagged on the end is the branch to Portland. A few surprises here too for, to begin with, there is no mention of Somerset & Dorset line trains, either via Wimborne or directly through Broadstone Junction, these being confined to the following Wimborne-

Bournemouth West table. Nor are any GWR trains shown (shewn?) between Dorchester Junction and Weymouth, despite traffic generally appearing on several other lines run jointly, irrespective of the company concerned. Perhaps it is because that stretch of line is GWR-owned though it seems strange the South Western thinks the GW only works between Weymouth and Portland!

Down trains Nos 148 and 150 are interesting as they form daily 'Through' workings by other companies. No 148 is headed 'Pass GW & GC' and leaves Eastleigh at 4.40pm, terminating at Bournemouth West at 6.6pm. Investigation shows this reached LSWR metals at Basingstoke at 3.52 (dep. 4.0pm) indicating it travelled via Reading and changed engines at Basing, the Great Western handing over responsibility there. The GC part of the ensemble presumably arrived at Reading via Woodford Halse, Banbury, Oxford and Didcot. No 150 is also a joint 'Pass' working but this time by the 'LN&W & GN'. This train, also destined for Bournemouth West with a 6.13pm arrival time, departs Eastleigh at 5.6pm. Its routing to the LSWR is another that could be replicated today, the LNW section arriving at Clapham Junction via Willesden and the West London Line. Its departure time is noted as 3.34pm

Totton & Eling station looking east back towards Redbridge and Southampton West.

but there's a footnote that reads, "This Train leaves No 1 Platform, Clapham Junction, at 3.25pm, and after attaching GN Coaches will leave East Box at 3.34pm". The departure arrangements, and particularly the specific mention of East Box, are such as to suggest there is a shunt move of some nature made here to gain the down side of the layout. It is possible the pointwork that may have been in place then could have provided direct access from the northernmost platforms of the station to what is now the Down Windsor Slow line though this move was certainly not possible in the 1900 track layout.

The Great Northern vehicles would almost certainly have come through Snow Hill to Blackfriars and then over the rather convoluted route to Clapham Junction via Loughborough Junction, the Catford Loop and Factory Junction. It is, of course, entirely possible the Tottenham & Hampstead Junction Joint would have seen them on to LNWR metals at Willesden Junction High Level and the West London from there. But as the Great Northern had been granted running powers over the ex-LCDR Metropolitan Extension in exchange for contributing toward the cost, that route is the much more likely one. Leaving from the Windsor side the train is noted as running to the main line via East Putney, an indication it was probably relatively lightly loaded. The steep climb up to the Putney Bridge-Wimbledon line was preceded by a turnout with a 20mph speed restriction at Point Pleasant Junction which

precluded a 'run' being taken at the gradient, though records indicate drivers often took a liberal view of such restrictions. In later days even a Bulleid 'Merchant Navy' usually required a pilot on this section when rostered for the 3.54pm Clapham Junction-Templecombe milk empties. That may, of course, have been how the 'joint' train was worked though the table makes no mention of a banker or pilot.

The return workings are also of interest, particularly of the GN/LNW train which has timing changes early in the timetable's life. Up to and including 10th July it departs Bournemouth West at 10.9am and on arrival at Central at 10.16 is attached to the 8.50 from Weymouth which arrived five minutes ahead of it. The portmanteau assemblage departs at 10.21 and is once more routed via East Putney for the 'through' portion to be detached on the Windsor side of Clapham Junction. However, from 12th July the 'joint' service runs as a separate train, leaving Bournemouth West at 10.5 and Central at 10.16 and running five minutes earlier throughout. Meanwhile the 8.50 up Weymouth is 12 minutes ahead of it, having omitted previously served stations between Dorchester and Wareham, and does not now make the hike round through East Putney. There are no variations for the GW/GC service which leaves Bournemouth West at 11.20am and runs independently throughout to Basingstoke, arriving at 1.18pm. As the Great Western takes over there, no departure time is shown.

The Wimborne-Bournemouth West timetable noted above has Waterloo and Bath as the two starting points. One interesting footnote on the weekdays up direction page reads, "These are the only Trains that convey Horses and Carriages for London", two of them in fact, departing Bournemouth at 6.40am and 12.35pm with Waterloo arrivals scheduled at 10.35am and 4.5pm respectively. There appears to be no such arrangement provided in the opposite direction, or at least none specified. Not surprisingly the Somerset & Dorset features strongly in this table with some very creditable times noted. The final piece of doubling of this quite magnificent railway, the eight miles between Blandford Forum and Corfe Mullen Junction, had only been completed in 1905. But no fewer than twenty-six miles of the sixty-four between Bath and Broadstone Junction were still single track and remained so until the line closed in March 1966. Among the highlights are the 2.13pm from Bath that took only 1hr 53m to get into Bournemouth West, with the 4.4pm not far behind, taking only five minutes more. Wimborne appears in the timings of some S&D passenger trains but most of them now by-pass it, running directly between Corfe Mullen and Broadstone Junction. Work in the up direction is, in general, not quite as impressive, though the 8.37am from Bournemouth West matches the best southbound runs with a Bath arrival scheduled at 10.27. However, even at this early stage the S&D did not run on Sundays.

The Somerset & Dorset features in the next two tables also, being summaries of the company's freight workings between Bath and Wimborne and of all its trains over that portion of the LSWR's Ringwood line between Wimborne and Wimborne Junction, where the S&D bore away toward Corfe Mullen Junction. There are no fewer than three down direction 'through' freight workings between Bath and Wimborne though all spend some time - fifty minutes the least, one hour longer the most - at Templecombe where, presumably, some re-marshalling takes place. The timing of the earliest one south of Templecombe is different on a Tuesday when it runs as part of the 2.50am off Bath, which thus becomes the 'through' train, but on other days forms a portion of the 2.0am down. The up direction table shows only one freight train running to Bath from Wimborne and this also spends more than an hour at Templecombe.

More byways follow: The Easton & Church Hope Railway on Portland precedes the Bishop's Waltham, a 3¾ mile branch from Botley on the Eastleigh-Fareham line, though dignified by having connections to/from Waterloo shown. After these come Cosham-Havant and the Lee-on-the-Solent Railway off the Gosport branch, before several pages covering Southampton-Fareham-Portsmouth including Gosport and Stokes Bay. Inter-company co-operation here too, with services from Bristol (dep Sarum 10.48am and 3.27pm) and Cardiff (dep Sarum 1.33pm and 7.30pm). The two earlier trains run to Portsmouth Harbour, the later pair terminating at the 'Town' station. Return

workings leave for Cardiff at 8.5am and 5.0pm and for Bristol at 12.20pm and 2.5, in all four cases working out of Portsmouth Town station. One other train inevitably draws today's eye: it departs from Fort Brockhurst at 11.38am and passes Fareham seven minutes later. The column is headed, 'Special with Discharged Solders As Required' but there is no indication whither it is bound!

Midland & South Western Junction services appear here and there in the Southampton to Salisbury timetable as, indeed, do those Bristol and Cardiff trains already noted. They appear again, as do MSWJ services, in the several pages of timetable covering the Andover-Southampton via Romsey line obliquely referred to when considering the Fullerton Motor. But after that comes a very important main line, the Portsmouth Direct. The first train out of Waterloo leaves at 5.20am, making calls at Weybridge, Woking, Guildford and Godalming and all stations thence. A footnote states a pilot is attached at Guildford to work the 7.20am from Haslemere. No mention is made here of the sort of locomotive this should be but it has to be assumed, were it not a tank engine, tender-first working would have been necessary from Guildford unless Haslemere had a turntable at the time, which seems doubtful. The 9.5am works non-stop over the Guildford New Line from Surbiton, and south of Guildford calls only at Haslemere, Fratton and Portsmouth Town, reaching Harbour station at 11.19am. If this seems a rather pedestrian schedule for the 75 miles of route, the competing Brighton, with an additional 13½ miles to cover, could almost match it though its trains were relatively light. The best was the late-afternoon service from London Bridge, the 70¾ miles to the first stop at Chichester being booked in 94 minutes. Portsmouth Harbour was reached 28 minutes later after calls at Havant, Fratton and Portsmouth Town.

No 26 down is another 'As Required' train, horseboxes running mid-morning between Woking and Petersfield. A footnote shows how much reliance was placed on local officials: ".....as arranged by the Agent at Woking who will instruct the Guard and arrange as to the Stations at which the Train shall call". How much notice was the Agent given, I wonder, to be sure the necessary vehicles were available at the required locations? A daily horsebox working is scheduled between the same two points in the early evening though in this case Milk Vans are attached.

Guildford cattle market obviously took place on Tuesdays for a cattle train is scheduled to leave Petersfield that day at 6.45am, picking up at all stations south of Godalming and reaching Guildford at 8.53. There appears to be no later and matching southward working specified but Guildford despatches a train of cattle that day at 5.5pm, calling at Woking, Weybridge and all stations to Surbiton to terminate at Wimbledon at 6.55. Whether the animals were destined for fattening or slaughter at these intermediate settlements is beyond the boundaries of this article. A cattle market ceased to operate in Guildford around 1999 but tradition is maintained by a Farmers Market held in the High Street on the first Tuesday of the month (*January excepted!*).

The 4.50pm up Midhurst-Woking goods, which joins the Portsmouth line at Petersfield, is another that has a footnote regarding cattle traffic, having to call at Milford on Petersfield market days to detach cattle if required. The timetable does not specify which day that is!

Havant and Cosham feature again in the next table which covers the triangle formed by those two points and Portsmouth. Besides South Western services this includes all the Brighton trains between the east and south junctions and although classed as a Summary occupies no fewer than six pages. Two more byways follow, the Midhurst branch and the short East Southsea line from Fratton. The latter was jointly owned by the South Western and Brighton but worked by one or other of the companies alternately for five years. The LSWR had begun this stint on 1st January 1908. (The joint owners decided to close the line within two weeks of the start of World War 1). The next table comes as a complete surprise though perhaps it should not be because it covers workings in the Isle of Wight along the section of railway the South Western also jointly owned with the Brighton between Ryde Pierhead and St Johns Road. The earliest train is the 3.30am Mail worked by the Isle of Wight Railway seven days a week. Oddly perhaps, the table is headed 'Ryde Pier Railway' though the section over water represents only one third of the total distance.

Another summary, this time between Guildford and Peasmarsh Junction comes next, covering the workings by all three Southern companies over this busy 1¾ miles of track. Following on is the table for that tight-knit group of lines between Guildford, Aldershot and Farnham. The SECR Reading-Redhill trains feature strongly in the ten pages of this table too, while dealing with the same vicinity are two pages for the Ascot-Aldershot-Farnham route with Waterloo figuring also. No 4 down, the 7.0am from Waterloo is interesting on two counts. Firstly, there is a stern warning at the foot of the page: "This Train will not convey Horses or Carriages to or from any Station". I'm tempted to add 'So there!' But what is more interesting is that this train is a Waterloo-Waterloo circular, made possible by the now vanished chord between Frimley Junction and Sturt Lane Junction. The train stands at Woking for eleven minutes and in that time is coupled to the 6.45am from Southampton which follows it in. The ensemble departs at 9.9 and gets into Waterloo at 9.47am having called only at Vauxhall. This method of working figures throughout the day, the 8.0am for example picking up a Portsmouth train at Woking and also making a dash for the capital thereafter with a similar interruption at Vauxhall. The system is practised in reverse too, the 2.28pm down shedding a Guildford portion at Woking and the 4.12pm being the trailing part of a Gosport train that traverses the Meon Valley line. The division takes place at Woking at 4.47pm. Vauxhall is ignored by these two though the 2.28

calls at all stations between Surbiton and Woking.

Now we return to suburbia, at least how we think of suburbia now, with the routes out to Leatherhead and Guildford. The first look at this table is astonishing simply by the relative paucity of traffic by today's standards though there is already strong evidence of growing commuter demand. The first up train from Leatherhead, for example, leaves at 5.8am but then there is a gap of over two hours, until 7.17. At the height of what is today's rush hour Leatherhead despatches trains to Waterloo at 7.52, 8.16 (ex-Bookham), 8.36, 8.54 (ex-Guildford) and 9.27 (ex-Horsley). Then there's another half-hour wait for the next one and an hour beyond that. (At the time of writing no fewer than fifteen trains leave Leatherhead for Waterloo between 0524 and 0924.)

The evening rush hour is similar with Waterloo departures for Leatherhead at 4.30, 5.25 (not Saturdays), 5.28 (slow from Wimbledon), 5.59, 6.32 and then another slower one at 6.34. Miss that and you've a wait until 7.8pm.

The table for the Joint line between Epsom and Leatherhead holds no surprises except that there are no references to the ultimate destinations of any of the trains. And quite understandably only LSWR down services have their departure times at Leatherhead shown. The companies retained separate stations here, it being left to the Southern to rationalise things by closing the South Western one from July 1927 and having all traffic use the ex-LBSCR station.

The Windsor Group follows and here there are some surprises but mainly in the way the various lines are laid out. Indeed, the tables are not specified as either 'Down' or 'Up' direction and close perusal makes it clear why. In the ostensibly 'down' direction table for example, which has Waterloo at the head, the up direction Woking-Byfleet Junction section is shown as a preliminary to Addlestone Junction/Weybridge-Staines [Junction]. The down Windsor branch times are below that but only onward from Staines High Street station. Thereafter the up direction continues through Ashford and Feltham and along the Hounslow Loop to Brentford where freight trains to and from the northern companies generally paused for a short time, probably for inspection and perhaps also for crew changes. Limited marshalling of freight trains took place at the sidings here though most of this was done for the South Western rather inconveniently and expensively at Willesden. Brentford sidings ceased to have such importance after Feltham Yard opened in stages from October 1920. The route then continues to Old Kew Junction where the North & South Western Junction Railway is joined to and through Acton Wells Junction and from there to other companies' marshalling yards at Neasden, Brent and Willesden.

There are naturally some interesting goods traffic workings here though, as in earlier tables, many such trains do not figure on every day of the week. There is, for example, a 2.30am departure from Woking headed *'1.15am Goods Guildford, not Mondays'* with an arrival at Willesden

T9 No 710, southbound at Swaythling. Clearly trespass is not just a present day phenomena.

timed at 4.5am. But on Mondays it starts from Woking at 2.30am and runs as a Cattle train to exactly the same timings, though a footnote states it "Will stop at Byfleet, Chertsey, Staines Junction, Feltham and Hounslow when required to take on Cattle for Maiden Lane". That station and sidings there were very close to the large and important Metropolitan Meat Market opened off the Caledonian Road by the City Corporation in 1855. This service also runs as a Cattle train on Sundays though it departs Guildford at 1.30am. From Woking the timings are exactly as for the Monday working except that there are no instructions about picking-up from intermediate stations *en route*.

The daily 9.26am goods from Woking spends half an hour at Staines before proceeding to Brentford, calling for twenty minutes at Feltham on the way. An hour's wait is scheduled at Brentford before departure for Willesden at 12.30pm but a footnote makes the probable reason for the stopover clear. "Wagons and Road Box Traffic by this Train for Twickenham, Richmond, Teddington, Kingston, and Stations on the Shepperton Line must be taken to Brentford and sent from the latter Station by the 1.37pm Goods, Brentford to Richmond". Another Goods train leaves Woking at 9.30am, right on the tail of the Willesden train but runs to a slightly slower schedule and stands at

Chertsey for twenty-five minutes before proceeding. This one, however, is destined for Reading, taking the now-lifted east to south curve at Virginia Water. While Willesden features most commonly as the northern destination, Brent receives a number of trains, almost all noted as 'Empty Wagons' emanating from such places as Woking, Wimbledon and Guildford. It may be safely assumed that the vehicles have been conveniently gathered at these starting points from stations in their vicinity and will be despatched from Brent to the East Midland coalfields for further supplies of domestic fuels. Brent is also the destination for the 1.0pm Goods from Eastleigh which spends thirty minutes at Woking before continuing. The enginemen are relieved at Feltham according to a footnote though only a passing time is recorded at the station. After 1½ hours at Brentford and a five-minute stop at Kew East Junction the train gets to Brent at 7.2pm. It is not only inter-company traffic that appears here for the 8.20pm Basing-Nine Elms Goods passes this way with the usual stops at Staines and Brentford, though it does not call at Woking. To follow the remainder of its journey into London one has to take up the timetable book for the Metropolitan District. Sunday naturally sees fewer trains but Salisbury features then, despatching a Goods at 2.0am which departs Woking at 5.20 and, having made the usual call at Brentford, gets to Willesden at 7.17am.

Southbound workings also rouse some interest, not least No 30, the 11.52am Willesden to Southampton, as it attracts no fewer than three separate footnotes. Instruction 'D' reads, "Stops at Hounslow on Mondays, when required, to take on Gunpowder for Southampton: and at Staines Junction, when necessary, to attach Cattle Traffic for Guernsey". One hopes that for their safety the cattle were well separated from the gunpowder! Then footnote 'F' states, "The load of this Train may be made up to 50 Vehicles at Brentford, including 20 Wagons of Coal or other heavy Minerals". Finally, according to instruction 'G', "Stops at Woking for examination only". The 9.18pm Willesden-Southampton Goods is also stopped at Woking only for examination but this train also has a specific instruction, that it, "Stops at Staines Junction to detach perishable Traffic only, for Windsor and Reading Lines". (As an aside, note the sometimes anomalous use of capital letters to lend weight to specific words in these instructions, a practice, incidentally, not confined to working timetables around this period.)

Finally in this section come four quite short timetables, the first being the Waterloo 'Roundabout' services. But here there is a hint of regular departures though still some quite large gaps between trains, even at what might be considered busy times. Late-afternoon anti-clockwise departures leave Waterloo at 4.15 (after a 1½ hour gap be it noted), 4.57, 5.18, 5.57, 6.18 and 6.35, which hardly comprises a rush-hour service, especially as the next departure is not until 7.30. The clockwise service is similarly bunched, but once more there is a gap exceeding one-and-a-half hours before the 4.52 departure, others following at 5.10, 5.35 fast to Norbiton *(SX)*, 5.38, 6.10, 6.52 and 7.20 and after that at 8.35. A regular interval hourly service is provided in both directions on Sunday.

The Brighton appears to hold the upper hand on the Ludgate Hill and Wimbledon line though confined to the section west of Tulse Hill: both routes from Tooting to Wimbledon – via Haydons Road and via Merton Abbey - are included. Passenger traffic was withdrawn from the latter line in 1929 though freight continued for many years more. The starting point in this table is Snow Hill, a reminder that the South Western was among contributors to the cost of the Chatham's Metropolitan Extension. The company also had running powers over the Brighton line between Tulse Hill and the start of the Joint line at Streatham South Junction. Most trains appear to be confined to the section but 'through' evening services to Kingston leave Ludgate Hill at 8.27 and 11.38. The second of these comes into Wimbledon via Merton Park, in other words requiring reversal for its onward journey. Sunday also sees workings to Kingston, at 9.47am, 1.42pm, 7.32 and 10.30 with an additional one at 4.35pm in June, superseded by a 4.25 departure from 4th July. These start from St Paul's. Oddly there are no up trains from Kingston

to Snow Hill on weekdays but a matching five on Sundays, at 8.30am, 12.30pm, 2.33, 5.50 and 8.54, all terminating at St Paul's. A summary of all trains between Tulse Hill and Streatham South Box follows, as though to emphasise the importance of this two-and-a-bit miles of shared line.

This District's Working Timetables are completed with a comprehensive compilation of trains over the West London Extension Line. This differs from all others in that only departure and passing times are shown and letters in the headings identify which company is running which train. 'S', 'B' and 'NW' need no explanation though a footnote makes clear that South Western trains terminate at Clapham Junction's platforms 1 and 2 while the Brighton and North Western companies' trains use the Brighton side of the station. One would have thought any signalman working Latchmere Junction box would have learned that very early in his training.

Just one other thing: the rift between Herbert Walker and Henry Holmes came about, at least in part, because Holmes had a chip on his shoulder. At the age of 49 he had confidently expected to succeed Sir Charles Owens as the South Western's General Manager and could not hide his resentment when the Board went instead for new blood from outside the confines of Waterloo. Walker, a London & North Western man who had learned his trade under G P Neele and Robert Turnbull, both exceptionally able Traffic men, took up office in January 1912. One of his first tasks was to revive the fortunes of the inner suburban services, failing due to increasing road competition. From his own experience of regular headway working he saw this as the way forward, especially when allied to a frequent service. Moreover, in July 1912, only months after taking office, Walker appointed Sir Alexander Kennedy as the South Western's electrification consultant, taking forward the idea that services should not only be regular and frequent but relatively fast and cheaper to run than was possible with steam power.

He had already noted the closely timed mid-morning bunch of West of England trains but as a preliminary to a complete recast of the timetable over the entire South Western system he met Holmes to discuss his plans for increasing patronage. Being well aware of Holmes's attitude toward him Walker finished the meeting by asking the Superintendent if he would kindly produce some draft regular interval timetables for the Kingston Roundabout service and let Walker have them a month hence. In due course Holmes reported that regular headway working was impossible on the South Western however much it might be practised on less busy railways. Walker's simple response was to transfer the timetable office out of Holmes's department and into a new section under his direct control.

And it wasn't just the timetable disagreement that caused further problems between the two men. Walker had early made a habit of touring the railway almost as an everyday passenger to see its staff at work. He became

The line that time forgot. Fort Brockhurst south of Fareham on the route to Gosport. Opened as the first branch line off the original London to Southampton railway, the terminus at Gosport was originally intended to serve Portsmouth across the other side of the harbour. With a direct rail connection later provided at Portsmouth and a poor by comparison London service from Gosport, it is no surprise the Gosport line succumbed as early at 1953. Seen here in April 1947 there are no obvious rail passengers and instead the lady may well be waiting for the rival bus service.

increasingly dissatisfied with some of the lax practices he found which determined him to tighten up the operation in general. That same year the whole operation was de-centralised, control over most things in their areas being given directly to District Superintendents, leaving Holmes and his department with a small rump of responsibility for accidents and setting fares and goods rates. Walker rearranged District boundaries and moved their operational centres to more logical locations. Because of the added responsibility each District had an assistant superintendent allocated to it, Walker, as was his way, personally picking the brightest young men from Holmes's staff to fill these positions.

In many respects the animosity between the two men was a pity, especially from Holmes's point of view. His regular interval holiday 'relief' services on the Bournemouth line, introduced as early as 1910, showed he had an appreciation of the benefits of such a system. Walker did not deny Holmes was a brilliant organiser as his part in the work of getting the BEF successfully to France in 1914 showed. But it was Holmes's own cussedness and sense of injustice that led to the truncation of his

responsibilities and his ultimate decision to retire in 1916 at the early age of 53 years. It may be significant that no apparent effort was made to get him to stay.

Walker was under no illusion about the difficulty of getting his passenger timetable plans to fruition. It eventually took four years for the 'mathematical timetable' to be completely brought into operation and the haphazard, maybe even bizarre 1909 efforts by Holmes and his predecessors firmly laid to rest. But I still find them extraordinarily interesting and entertaining!

Apart from the source volume I have also made some use of the following: Jowett's Railway Atlas of Great Britain and Ireland, History of the Southern Railway (Dendy Marshall), Sir Herbert Walker's Southern Railway (Charles Klapper), The South Western Railway (Hamilton Ellis), The London & South Western Railway (O S Nock), Railways of the Southern Region (Geoffrey Body), British Railway History 1830-1876 (Hamilton Ellis), Lines Around Wimbledon (Vic Mitchell & Keith Smith), Rail Centres, Clapham Junction (J N Faulkner), The West London Joint Railways (J B Atkinson), The London & North Western Railway (O S Nock), The Somerset & Dorset Railway (Robin Atthill), Railway Track Diagrams no 5, Southern & TfL (ed Gerald Jacobs) and LBSCR Table of Distances Jan 1901.

FROM SCHOOLBOY TO SIGNAL BOX

THE MEMORIES OF BILL TRIGG

Part 3

(Continued from Issue No 20)

I was eighteen in September 1949 and had to register for national service. Perhaps not surprisingly I requested to be allowed to join the Royal Engineers - as indeed did most of the boys employed as signal lads – since we hoped to be posted to the Longmoor Military Railway. Of course at the time, you could never be certain which regiment you would be "invited" to join! I always thought it strange that our Area Inspector gave me an instruction before I was called up, "When you get to Longmoor, see Major Ratledge, head of Railway Training, tell him you're one of Walters' boys".

I started my fourteen weeks' basic training at Cove, near Farnborough. The camp here was alongside the railway line, whilst across the road was the Aircraft Research Establishment. At that time they were engine testing and test flying the Meteor jet, a blessing for us recruits, as the noise from the aircraft made orders by the Drill Instructors impossible to hear and so prevented us from square-bashing.

Having completed basic training I was indeed posted to Longmoor, although I did not seek out Major Ratledge - not the done thing for a lowly Sapper to do. At Longmoor I was informed I was to attend a

'Blockman' (signalman) course, which would last for three months. Unfortunately one course had started just before my arrival, and before the next I was detailed to general fatigue duties, which consisted mainly, in my case, of unloading by hand locomotive coal briquettes, each weighing about fourteen pounds, from coal wagons adjacent to the locomotive coaling dock. We new arrivals seemed to get this job every day, as there were fatigue men there who knew just where to stand at the muster, ready for the best work. I assumed these chaps were professionals who were content to see their time out doing what they did. It was a bit like the Mafia in uniform.

Unloading loco coal was not too bad to start with, as it was what the CSM termed "a task" which meant that when you had finished your allotted duty, you were finished for the day, so I would have a shower, change and down to Liss on the afternoon "Bullet", the Military railway passenger train, or by the Liss and District Bus Company's bus to catch the Portsmouth and Southsea stopping service to Surbiton at a cost of four shillings and three pence using a railway privilege form (these had to be authorised in advance by your original station master so it was a case of

153 Railway Op. Squad at Longmoor. Bill is fourth from the left in the back row.

always having a signed form ready for use).

The Liss and District bus company, which was one of those local services that I think is sadly missed today. If there were about a dozen of us waiting at the camp bus stop, with no Bullet due, a phone call to the bus office would have an additional vehicle arrive within minutes. On the regular service the driver provided a door-to-door collection and delivery service for the locals, whilst all the time we would be looking at our watches to see if there was still a chance of catching the London train. Many a time we would hear the bus driver say something like, "Can't go yet, Mrs Brown always catches this one". Despite such delays, rarely did we miss the train.

This routine of fatigues continued for about a month or two, an important part of the duty being to carry one briquette a day back to the barrack block for use on the fire. This would supplement the issue of fuel, which was a simple scuttle of coke per day. With men on different shifts the barrack room fire could be lit all day.

One day I called at the company office to enquire when my Blockman's course was due to begin: the heaving of briquettes of coal was strenuous work and after a full day it, you were really only any good for a shower and lying on your bed to sleep. To my surprise my name was not on the Blockman's course and instead was against a Brakesman - Shunter's course to start the following Monday. (The Army referred to Guards as Brakesmen.) This course lasted from 4-6 weeks and on satisfactory completion of it, it was a requirement to work all the turns in rotation: there were six of these, lettered A to F.

Using "A" as an example, this was the passenger service with No.600 *Gordon* and the very nice South Eastern birdcage three-coach set. When I first did this duty I made a silly mistake for I did not know that haversack rations were provided automatically as the turn was rostered for more than eight hours. These rations consisted of two doorstep-size sandwiches. one of cheese and one of marmalade, plus an apple (at least the apple was edible!) But because I did not draw the ration, I was up before the O/C on defaulters for wasting government food. When asked what I had done for food, I explained I had gone up to Maggie's, the café just up the road from Oakhanger station, when on that leg of the duty.

Maggie's was a regular haunt for the various duties that arrived at Oakhanger. The Blockman there could be relied upon to mount the cab of the yard shunting engine, which would be screwed down at the siding buffers. and give a blast on the whistle should there be any unexpected traffic – usually in the form of the petrol powered Wickham car that the officer in charge of the line (usually a sergeant) would use to travel around the system. As this had to be signalled, there was always ample warning available so everyone would look busy upon his arrival.

For my rations offence I was given two days "confined to barracks", which involved parading at the guard room at 7.00 pm for playing of the "retreat" and again at eight and nine o'clock in whatever part of the camp the MPs decided you should turn out in. Otherwise it would be a task like peeling potatoes in the cookhouse – and there were always plenty of those vegetables to attend to. Fortunately I knew one of the camp police, a quiet chap who was from Nine Elms loco. When I was not under 'his charge' he and I spent hours of free time playing cribbage. We would walk down to the Woolmer Hotel, a bit off the beaten track from the camp and quite often we would be invited to play a hand of crib by the old chaps in the bar, either as a pair or, to make up their four if they were one short. It was all good fun. I recall they were very generous to two poorly-paid Sappers.

Clearly there must have been some military connection with the pub for there was the well-known sign over the bar commenting never to volunteer for anything in the Army.

Speaking of Nine Elms, my friend recalled the time a driver had left Nine Elms with his engine to run light, ready for the 5.40 am Waterloo to Weymouth. This duty regularly saw a number of locomen who had been on nights using the engine as a means of getting a lift to Waterloo ready to catch services to their homes. The trouble was that on this occasion there were so many he did not notice one particularly important person was missing – his own fireman. He said it was a bit embarrassing to have to telephone the shed foreman and report that there was no fireman present!

Apart from the one passenger duty at Longmoor, all the other turns were freight or shunting duties. I don't remember now the full details, but one was the Longmoor pilot, that pottered about with movements in the Yard and out on the Longmoor Downs and sometimes as far as Applepie sidings that ran parallel to the Greatham road after crossing the Woolmer road.

Another was the shunt at Woolmer exchange sidings, which was the marshalling yard of the LMR and I think it was "F" that went into the large REME depot at Oakhanger, called Halifax sidings. I remember the first time I was on this duty; we came out of Longmoor yard, 0-6-0ST and brake-van. As this was the first duty of the day the driver was in possession of the one engine in steam key. We steamed through the platform at Longmoor Downs where there was a group of sappers at the platform end, who I noticed were all waving at both the engine crew and myself as we passed through at ever-increasing speed. I recall thinking what a friendly bunch they were. One was John Rowbottom, an ex-Hampton Court Junction booking boy, a little older than me, who had arrived at Longmoor earlier. He was already passed out as a blockman, as indeed were most of this little group.

It later transpired they were waiting to board the brake-van ready to open up the line, for the normal day's workings to begin, at which point the one engine in steam key would be withdrawn.

Instead they had to be provided with a lorry to get

Bill at Hampton Court Crossing which survived until 1957.

them to work, whilst the officer in charge had to come into the Halifax depot to retrieve the one engine in steam key; before normal working could be started. No names appeared on Part One orders for this incident, so I assume it was considered to be a good training exercise.

One other duty to mention was that which went down the goods line to Bordon to meet the British Railways freight each day and collect traffic for the Longmoor system. This involved a cup of tea and a game of crib in the SR signal box waiting for the train to arrive from Aldershot. When it did, the procedure was for the army engine to couple up to the BR brake van which would then be knocked off into an empty siding. We would then pick up any wagons for the LMR, re-attach the BR van, assemble our train so the brake van was at the rear and then take the wagons to Oakhanger for sorting. Usually the vehicles consisted of loaded vans for the various REME depots, loco coal for Longmoor, plus a steady supply of household coal for the Louisburg siding at Oakhanger from which domestic coal was provided for the married quarters at Bordon.

Having experienced all the duties through to 'F' my name went up on orders for seven days leave followed by a posting to Germany. Various experiences, road and railway, followed and I was eventually returned to Barton Stacey transit camp and 'demob'. This last episode lasted just ten days and I will freely admit it was the worst ten days of my army life. It was February with frost and snow on the ground, we were housed in Nissen huts but these had no window frames, I assume they had been burnt by previous

occupants on the slow combustion stove in an unsuccessful effort to keep warm. The stove had a short length of flue pipe, but this did not reach the height of the roof: so even assuming there was some kindling to be found to light the issue coke there were fumes to contend with. I would go to bed with my issue greatcoat over the blankets only to wake in the morning with a layer of snow over everything. To add insult to injury a barrack room inspection resulted in pay being stopped for damage to the windows. That was to be the end of my military career although I was still required to sign on for three years in the Army Emergency Reserve where I was assigned to 153 Railway Operating Company. This entailed attendance at two weeks' camp at Longmoor for each of the next three years.

The reward for two years army service was twenty-four days demob leave: so I reported to the staff office at Woking, to inform them I was home and looking for work. I was allocated to learn the signal box at Hampton Court Crossing, a grade 4 Porter / Signalman post, the training time to include something like six weeks classroom work in a wooden hut down where the line to Guildford leaves the main line at Woking.

This building doubled as the signal and shunting school and I did both courses. The shunting school involved some days out, to Effingham Junction for instruction in coupling the old suburban electric stock with torpedo ends, and across to Reading Southern for freight work (use of a shunting pole) and on coupling instruction for steam-hauled passenger stock: how to throw up a Buckeye coupling weighing some 56lbs, and get the pin in. At Reading, and mainly because the tutor was keen on all things Great Western, we were there in time to see the down Cornish Riviera Express go majestically through Reading General on its way to the west.

The original signal box at Hampton Court Crossing had met with an accident in October 1947, having been knocked down during a shunt move from the long sidings located on the up side of the line. Some electric units were intended to go out on to the up line and then back into the platform to form a passenger service to Waterloo. It was a foggy day and it seems the shunter heard the clank of a signal move and assumed it was the ground signal for the move. Instead it was the running line signal for a late-running passenger service. The result was that the shunter gave the motorman the signal to start: so the motorman, who

Post-1957 a new box was provided at the crossing and which subsequently took over the function of the former station box a year later.

The similarly named Hampton box but on the line between Twickenham and Shepperton. This standard LSWR design structure had just six levers and was operational from 1878 until 1975.

was located at the Hampton Court station end of the units, set off, but only got just beyond the points which were still set for the very short shunting neck. The end of the line was marked by the running rails being bent up at ninety degrees with no proper stop block. Even so these bent rails did their job; for instead of the units going out on to the main line they ran into the signal box, knocking it over into Summer Lane.

The signalman on duty was Jack Kingman who escaped without injury, although naturally he suffered from shock. He later progressed to become an area Inspector, and was also an enthusiastic First Aider who ran the Twickenham class.

The Wimbledon building department had to erect a makeshift signal box rapidly; basically it was a ground-level shed cobbled together out of various odd bits and pieces. The Signal & Telegraph department installed a knee frame and gate wheel providing communication with Hampton Court Junction or Thames Ditton one way and to Hampton Court station box the other. Train signalling was by Preece Open Block instruments, consisting of what we called the 'beer handle' to give permission for a train to approach and a wooden case with a miniature signal in it which when lowered was the authority to send a train forward. The starting signals here were thus free, hence the term 'open block' the alternative being 'lock and block' where the starting signals was locked until 'line clear' had been received from the signal box in advance. There were about 10 levers provided with special instructions provided for shunting between the station and crossing signal boxes as

these were less than a quarter of a mile apart.

The normal off-peak service was three trains an hour, leaving Hampton Court at 03, 25 and 43 minutes past the hour plus additional trains for race traffic to Hurst Park Races. (There were twenty-plus specials for the Whit Monday meeting - meaning a fair number of turns of the gate wheel!)

The box was open from 5.15 am to 12.40 am, a signalman working the 5.15 am to 12.35 pm and late turn 5.20 pm to 12.40 am turns. The porter / signalman worked the missing hours in the box with the remaining time on the platform.

From 21 June to 5 July 1952 I was at the first of my two-week camps back at Longmoor. The first week was a refresher of military matters, being taken up with military training on the rifle range which I always enjoyed, the usual square bashing and also what was termed "field craft". As might be imagined, this entailed crawling about on the ground with bits of twig and such like in the netting of your steel helmet. Without managing to kill or maim our colleagues we all managed to progress through to the second week.

At this stage we took over the railway and on this first camp I was assigned to a shunting gang at the Woolmer exchange sidings together with a fellow conscript who was employed by the Port of London as a locomotive fireman. There was also a man called Charlie, a Z reservist from the war years, normally employed at Whitemoor Yard as the No1 on a shunt gang. Charlie tended to disappear into the high grass for long periods to rest although we could hardly blame him as he had done his bit during the war. I remember we had the usual J94 type 0-6-0ST with the crew having a bit of trouble getting it to steam. The chap from the PLA, I think his first name was Peter, enquired what the driver did in civilian life, and was told he was a baker. Hence we had a change round, our mate did the driving, and brought the fire round, and the driver was happy to do the wagon chasing.

I remember one day we had to parade, I think it was the Queen's Birthday and the part one orders said "medals will be worn". Old Charlie turned up with four or five dirty ribbons sewn on his tunic, and when asked why he had no medals, he produced another handful of ribbons from his top pocket saying, they were too heavy to carry to camp. Clearly he had seen a lot of service.

While at camp, I volunteered to play cricket for 153, in a game against 157, the locomotive squadron. Whilst fielding the ball came my way once and I went down on one knee with hands together in an attempt to gather it, only to see it literally disappear before my very eyes. It transpired it had gone down one of the holes provided for the rugby posts. I adopted a prone position, but could not reach the ball in the bottom of the hole, in the meantime the batsmen were chasing back and forth. I don't know how many runs were made before it was decided that we had a lost ball situation, and someone with very long arms was finally able to retrieve it. The game was eventually finished as a draw.

Back at Hampton Court Crossing I recall one particular train working. This was steam-hauled from Oxford and was a schools' educational trip using a Southern engine. Behind were between 10 to 12 coaches for which a turnover engine had to be provided. Upon arrival it ran into number two platform which was the continuation of the down line. With no engine release crossover, the turnover engine was used to take the stock back to Clapham Junction, whilst the train engine, when released, departed to Nine Elms for servicing. A similar operation was used for the return working.

On early turn we would meet the daily freight train that arrived from Surbiton. The first job was to run the engine round which could be done within the long sidings with just enough room to stand the engine, normally a '700', between the hand points and the ground signal. Then we would shunt the yard placing the new arrivals as necessary. The little engine shed was used by the new works department and any wagons for them were placed in that area, which entailed another run round. The return to Surbiton was around 10.35 am.

After this and until it was time to relieve in the box, duties were various but always included station cleaning. On the days when there was racing at Hurst Park this included collecting tickets until meal-break for an hour at 11.35 am and starting in the signal box at 12.35 pm.

One brief conversation I remember on a race day; was with the flamboyant tipster Prince Monolulu (real name Peter Carl McKay), always dressed in Indian style clothes and with his trademark saying, "I gotta an Orse". When I collected his ticket I asked for his tip for the day, instead he took me to one side and said, "If I knew what was going to win, do you think I would be dressed in this garb?" It was a good lesson.

Late turn week started at 12.35 pm with the evening station work assisting with the business service which included reducing the trains from eight cars to four, and shunting the not-required sets to berth in the sidings ready for the next day.

By the autumn of 1952 I had been promoted to one of the signalman's posts proper and was there when the smog came down on the 5th December 1952. It lingered for weeks, not finally dispersing until March by which time some 12,000 people had died, although official government figures put two thirds of these down to seasonal flu.

Because of the reduced visibility the crossing gates would be shut against the road, for very long spells once Hampton Court Junction had given 'train in section'. With visibility down to 2-3 yards it was necessary to keep the signal box door open and listen for the noise of the approaching train that might have missed the home signal so one had to be prepared to nip smartly out with a hand lamp in the hope that it would be seen. Luckily most drivers found the gas lamps of the crossing, and would then ask if it was all right to proceed into the station. At this stage most times it was not, so we would tell him to wait where he was until we gave him the authority to go forward. Meanwhile cars would arrive with a bump into the gates and the driver might be heard to say, "I think we are in the railway goods yard" or "this is a dead end". The thing I recall most about this period was how quiet everything was as the smog would deaden sound.

I remember one evening on late turn, when I needed to replace one of the gas mantles in the down side gas-lamp (the crossing had a stepladder provided). I had already positioned the steps when the down train was given as 'in section' by Hampton Court Junction. I went back to the box and dealt with the train, which passed me at normal speed. Before I could get back to my gas lamp repair the telephone was ringing and when I answered it was the driver of the down train. He commented he thought he had hit something when passing over the crossing. I had a look and found the step ladder broken into small pieces, ideal kindling for the box fire. I advised the poor motorman what had happened, as he feared he had hit a person. For my part I never did let on as to what happened to the stepladder, theft was assumed.

I had the misfortune to oversleep one morning and arrived at 5.25 am. As a result the first up train was delayed by three minutes. I reported the fact and was asked by the station master for an assurance it would not happen again. I replied I could promise but did say I had bought a new alarm clock and hoped this would solve the problem. He seemed satisfied with the response.

'A Rose amidst the Thorns'
READING SOUTH

Nick Deacon records his own memories and those of former Reading South fireman Roger Latch

Cushioned between the SECR and GWR railway bridges passing above Vastern Road in Reading, the shed entrance at Reading South typified many that were described in the yearly editions of 'The British Locomotive Shed Directory' compiled by Aidan Fuller. Here at Reading South his oft repeated phrase "…..the shed entrance is a gate……" was far too grandiose a term to describe what was merely a gap in the age weathered and much creosoted timbers that served as the main pedestrian access. Perhaps years ago there may well have been a gate but it matters not. I must have passed this 'gate' hundreds of times from about 1952 onwards, as alongside the fence was the public path taken by my family when walking to the riverside delights of the Thames at Kings Meadow or the promenade (locally referred by the obvious term the 'prom') at Caversham.

Through this proverbial hole in the fence, the brief view of the 'cinder path' (another of Fuller's regular descriptions of a feature now enshrined in railway lore) and the looming tenders of parked locos engendered a passion that remains with me to this day.

It was probably the very frustration of those anonymous tender ends (at Reading South such types were always positioned facing east and therefore away from the gate) that sparked the first in a long line of shed 'bunks' that would stretch all the way up until August 1965.

Despite an early demotion to sub-shed level and the loss of the loco allocation to Guildford and Redhill in 1954, the shed retained a healthy level of activity until the final days of steam on the Redhill line. Even allowing for this relegation I was always pleased to note its continued appearance within the pages of Aidan Fuller's work, qualifying as it did under his prefaced comment of "in the case of sub-sheds, directions are only given to the large and important ones". Well said Mr Fuller, you obviously knew that at Reading South size wasn't everything!

The 1860s SER Reading shed, even before it became a constituent of the SECR and then later part of the SR, always appeared to be poking an impertinent finger up at the magisterially disapproving GWR riding high upon its Brunellian bowling green as it swept past into Reading

General. The pomp and circumstance of the 115 lever GWR East Main box with rumoured infrastructure of an alleged million bricks seemed to turn its back upon the unseemly antics occurring immediately below it, rather in the manner of a prim Edwardian schoolteacher when suddenly confronted with the curves and flounces of some outrageous music hall turn. Typifying the contrast between the conformity of the GWR and its loco design were the handsome Wainwright 4-4-0s of the B1, F1, and D classes that could be seen on shed into the 1950s. During the same period D1, E1 and T9 4-4-0's also made the occasional appearance as well as M7 0-4-4T's that were drafted in from time to time when the south turntable was out of action. The pre-group feel to the place was further enhanced with examples of E3, E4, G6 , R1 and T1 'tankies' appearing on the 1950s allocations. But as mentioned, a gradual run-down began in 1954 when most of the shed's allocation were transferred to Redhill and Guildford. However, the shed retained its '70E' coding until briefly in 1959 when it inappropriately became a sub-shed of Basingstoke (70D). Waterloo must have realised their error as from 1960 and until the end Guildford (70C) was the parent depot. Despite the obvious demotion in status the shed remained busy almost until the end – indeed at times visitors would find it hard to credit that they were walking around a mere sub-shed such was the level of activity and numbers of occupants.

At Reading General not much seemed to change, other than the age of some of the engines. Few went spotting at Reading South except to take the occasional picture. But as a young spotter across the road in the late 1950s I used to watch with goggle-eyed fascination as ancient trespassers in the shape of Class 700 'Black Motors' or Class 'C' 0-6-0s would stagger across the pointwork under East Main to disappear almost apologetically behind the Platform 8 buildings with lengthy goods trains. On other occasions strange shapes showing a lot of 'leg' in the form of Q1s 'Charlies' - we Reading spotters called them 'coffee-pots' whilst unlike other parts of the country we did not use the derogatory term 'spam-cans', to describe the magnificent

Bulleid and Riddles designs 'on-shed'.

Class 700 or 'Black Motor' No 30697 of 1897 vintage is seen on the shed turntable at an unknown date – possibly before 20 April 1955 as this is when the loco moved from Guildford to its last shed Exmouth Junction. The turntable was often a casualty requiring lengthy repairs resulting in loco's having to use the 'table at Reading GWR shed or having to turn on the Reading West triangle. One of the last of the class to survive, No 30697 was withdrawn from 72A in November 1962 but was recalled to duty during the long Winter of '62/3. She vegetated at 72A until the end of the year not reaching Eastleigh for scrapping until January 1964.

BB and WC Pacifics - would inch crab-like through the up main centre road and shudder to a bad tempered halt before disappearing down the incline of the '1899 Connection' to the South yards. Of these, there were two sizable locations. one being the quaintly named 'Pug's Hole' sidings situated between the shed and the main line. Not surprisingly the 'Dunkirk' sidings, were a wartime addition in the early 1940s. A dash of modern Southern Railway power appeared from 1960 with the eventual arrival of six School 4-4-0s split between Guildford and Redhill. They were daily visitors to Reading until December 1962 when the last of the class were withdrawn.

Reading South shed always had a style of its own and just like the bond of a close family, many of its drivers, firemen, cleaners and locomotives remained connected to the depot in this fashion until the very end of steam. By pure fluke it was in this 'family' that the young Roger Latch

found himself while awaiting a suitable opening for a career as an engineer in the Merchant Navy. In the summer of 1963 and having found that there were no vacancies at Reading WR shed (81D), Roger tried his luck at Reading South. After a successful medical at the Regional M.O. at London Bridge station he was accepted for employment as a cleaner, under the wing of the current shed foreman at Reading South, Fred Marshall.

Quite expecting to spend some time at the bottom and distinctly muckier end of the grade, to his surprise his actual cleaning experience only extended to one locomotive before he was rapidly elevated to the 'passed cleaner' grade. "I even remember the number", he recalls. "It was N class 31866 which had been stopped for a number of weeks at the back of the shed by the WR East signal box". The difficulties that the Southern Region had in retaining experienced footplate men meant that the process of advancement – even for a self-confessed 'likely lad' like Roger - was always going to be pretty meteoric especially when compared to the WR across town where you could be in your forties and still only a fireman. (The reason why there were no vacancies just a few hundred yards away is not explained, although there may have been a reluctance to move away to gain promotion.) On the Southern, you could at a pinch be a 'passed fireman' at 23 and, like some young God, you were literally 'flying' with the world at your feet. Much of the rivalry between WR and SR men was still an extension of pre-nationalisation differences, some of the WR men, especially those with growing families to support, could be understandably touchy about the considerable difference in promotion prospects. Indeed Roger recalls a certain amount of low-level animosity. These differences were to ensure a permanent 'distance' between the two respective sets of men, a situation that lasted until the end of steam. In this vein Roger remembers that WR men resented the occasional visits of SR locos requiring attention if the

facilities at the south were 'on the blink'. WR fitters were, as he puts it, "less than happy trying to cope with 'foreign' motive power and their answer to everything seemed to be to burn it with a flare torch or whack it with a very substantial hammer' (to be fair probably a lot of steam repairs were actually conducted like this in the latter days anyway). Adding fuel to this situation was the confusion over driving positions. SR engines might be left or right hand drive dependent upon their age and origins. Later SR engines were of course all left hand whilst WR machines were 100% right hand drive.

Out of operational necessity there had to be some close liaison between the regions, although Roger remembers one situation later in his career that seemed to underline the persisting difference to the point of organised lunacy. Reading South yard shunts over the years had used locomotives of various classes, R1, G6, E4, Drewry 204hp diesels and latterly Guildford based 350hp diesels. Routine maintenance was carried out at Guildford as and when

This view of Reading South of 5 December 1948 shows repainting of the attractive SER canopy valancing in progress. One of the Waterloo 2 or 4-BIL electrics is seen to the left at platform 4. Platform 3 is blocked by a parcels van to provide access height for the painters to reach the canopies. Platform 2 possibly contains a B1 or F1 which were still regular performers on the Redhill services, while N No 31857, a Redhill engine at the time, prepares to remove stock from platform 4. To the right is Reading General with a Hall 4-6-0 about to depart from platform 5. The Hall has the early 'Ferret and Dartboard' on her tender that may suggest a slightly later date to the picture as this emblem was not introduced until late 1948 at the earliest. The cast iron platform lamps on their turned posts were a typically high Victorian statement soon to be replaced by the more prosaic SR concrete embellishments seen in the following photograph. Cam Camwell

A quiet moment at Reading South suggesting a post – September 1961 view when the station was renamed 'Reading (Southern)'. On the left a 4-HAL electric unit is stabled opposite Platform 1 while locomotive stock awaits movement from platforms 3 and 4 and also the stabling road at far right. The station often seemed to slumber for long periods such as this and then with a sudden flurry would awaken as Redhill and London services vied with one another in sudden bursts of activity. Also seen here is the wooden protective shuttering protecting the third rail from inadvertent human contact. Many were the tales where this protection was insufficient - much to the detriment of steam loco crews incautiously handling long fire irons or injudiciously using the tender waste water pipe to fill up a bucket of water for a wash.

required. This was arranged into any 'small hours' shift, the low speed capability of the shunters travelling any distance meaning night moves would thus avoid delays to traffic. One has to imagine the time it took to grind all the way to Guildford (and back) 'light engine' at a speed that was not going to exceed much more than 15mph. Remarkably the same trip also had to be undertaken when refuelling was required as there were no diesel fuel facilities at Reading South. "I was amazed that there were no working arrangements to allow for a short trip over to 81D to use the facilities there. Being denied this, the Southern depot was inconvenienced by a farcically wasteful exercise". But every cloud has a silver lining, the upside to this duty being that the fireman (more accurately the 'second-man') could catch up with some shut-eye on the cab floor.

Returning to Roger's time and before he could think of footplate work, he had to attend a statutory four-week course at the Fireman's School then located at Woking. There were was also regular attendance at the Mutual Improvement Classes held locally. Successful completion of these saw Roger attain the 'passed cleaner'

grade in the autumn of 1963 and after no more than eight weeks of railway employment!

By this time the menu of steam locomotives that worked out of Reading South had contracted to the types that would see out the remainder of the depot's existence – by now only two summers away. A snapshot of Guildford's steam allocation for the autumn of 1963 tells us that just six classes were on the strength, a total of 32 engines. These were: 3xBR Class 4 2-6-4Ts, 12xU 2-6-0s, 4xN 2-6-0s, 2xQ 0-6-0s, 10xQ1 0-6-0s and a solitary USA 0-6-0T. By the spring of the following year the loco strength would be augmented by the arrival 8xBR Class 4 2-6-0s and 4xIvatt LMS 2MT 'Mickey Mouse' 2-6-2Ts, the Q1s having in turn diminished to just four examples. Also seen at Reading South at this time were members of the large stud of S15 locos based at Feltham. In October 1963 the allocation stood at 18 or so but this number was to halve by the following year. Roger was to see footplate time on most of these types, particularly the N, U, S15 and Q1 designs.

As a new fireman in 'Goods Link 2', Roger fired for most of the old hands, many who would later see steam out on the Reading – Redhill services. 'Link 2' also had a number of 'as required' turns where cover for holidays, sickness and vacancies was needed and which in turn gave the opportunity to experience a reasonable amount of 'Link 1' passenger work. Roger recalls. "In particular, I remember firing for George Frampton on his very last trip on a Reading – Redhill service before he retired".

The perennial shortage of staff at Southern Region London depots also meant that there was a regular slice of remunerative loan work to be had, for Roger this meant at both Nine Elms and Guildford. "Loan work at Nine Elms could be anything; from preparation and disposal, Clapham Junction - Waterloo ECS, stopping, semi-fast and fast passenger work as far as Salisbury on the west of England line and even on down to Bournemouth. Basically, you never knew what you were going to end up with until you signed on!"

"Guildford was similar but obviously on a much smaller scale and I can remember quite a few passenger trips to Horsham and a couple of 'all-nighters' on PW trains, one just up the main line to Worplesdon and another on the Effingham Junction line in addition to prepping and disposing of the locomotive used. One late evening job I remember well was going 'on the cushions' to Woking, relieving on a Waterloo – Salisbury semi-fast as far as Basingstoke, going to the shed, preparing an engine, shunting the yard, bringing a goods back to Woking, being relieved there and catching a van train back to Guildford in the early hours of the morning". "Why do I remember this particular trip? Because the lighting in the Guard's compartment of the van train was not very good as I perched down on what I thought was a long trunk. It was only when we got to Guildford that the guard took great delight to inform me that my seat was in fact a coffin complete with a corpse! "All in a day's work" seemed quite an understatement!"

Link 2 duties were a hang-over from the labyrinthine working patterns of pre-nationalisation days. The most arduous of these were pick-up goods work with shunting at various locations, Earley, Wokingham, Bracknell, Ascot, Sunningdale, Bagshot and Camberley. Roger remembers the worst of these being a (very) early am turn from Reading to and from Sunningdale. Although by this stage of the 1960s many of the smaller feeder businesses with their own sidings were rapidly disappearing from the railway map, particularly the brickwork kilns that studded this area, there remained just enough of them to justify this type of duty for a little while longer. The Shell BP oil depot sidings at Earley were one of the last of these locations in the area and continued to generate revenue for the railway into the 1970s. Recollecting an average book-off time from this duty at around 10.30am, Roger wryly adds, "If you were lucky that is. But then that was the job and you just got on with it!"

"Another heavy duty was the 9.33am Reading – Guildford – Redhill goods rostered for a U or N on '38

equal to 52' which was asking a lot of a run-down 2-6-0. Reading to Redhill and back was measured as a 96 mile, 8 hour duty and qualified as a complete turn. A similar duty was a Reading Spur to Feltham goods turn".

"No. 1 Link, although responsible for the passenger duties (19 weekday departures and 9 Sundays), was also responsible for the main goods turn of the day, the 2.10pm Reading Spur to Redhill and a late afternoon van train to Waterloo (at 5.20pm I think). Reading men would work this service as far as Twickenham where they would swap with Nine Elms men working the Waterloo – Reading South van train".

"If I remember correctly No 1 Link consisted of about twelve sets of men and Link 2 a similar number. There was no connection with motormen employed on the 'juice' electric services to and from Waterloo. These men signed on at Reading South station and were regarded very much as 'a breed apart'. They were all ex-steam drivers and indeed counted many ex-Reading South men among their number, they could in practice be called back to perform their former duties if required. I imagine this would have been unpopular given the cleanliness and relative comfort of the electric units.

There was also a facility in place known as the 'dual link' where steam men had been trained up to drive electric units, but then had to wait for vacancies to occur. However, in my time I don't recall any steam men 'moving across', implying that there were few vacancies up for grabs at the time".

"Link 2 was also responsible for loco preparation and disposal. These required passed cleaners to carry out the full range of duties of a fireman and sometimes this also included 'loco prep'. I vividly remember being responsible for 'prepping' WC No 34037 'Clovelly' on an almost unheard of visit of the class to the shed. This was in December 1963. The loco had been 'stopped', I can't remember why, and then spent almost two weeks on shed before repairs were completed to enable its return home. At the time it was allocated to Eastleigh shed."

"Loco 'prep' included making sure that certain tools and effects were present such as shovel, bucket, brush, coalpick, hammer, spanners, various lamps, spare glasses, detonators, flags and indicator boards. Lamps were checked, topped up and trimmed, the sanding gear examined and boxes filled. The fire was to be made up, water level in the boiler checked, firebox and smokebox checked that there were no leaking tubes and the brick arch was OK. The water level in the tender was to be checked, coal trimmed, footplate cleaned, hydrostatic lubricators filled (where present) and route indicator discs and lamps placed in the correct position for the loco's next duty" This work was no different to that of the larger sheds and although Roger remembers the dirt, hard graft and difficult working conditions he accepted it all quite cheerfully. On his side was youth and, as he puts it, "at the time I was also a bit of a 'Jack the lad', fond of a good time and burning the candle at

This signal box simply described as 'Reading' is in fact 'Reading Junction' signal box and was situated in the fork of the up and down GWR lines (The 'Old Bank' of 1899 connecting the GWR and SECR lines) and the SR running lines to the east of the station. A second box of similar vintage was situated at the station throat to control movements there. The line in front of the box was officially known as the loco siding and the one just seen to the right the up siding west. The box opened in 1899 and replaced two other boxes known as No.1 and No. 2. A new frame was fitted in the box c. 1935. The arches mark the point where a connecting line passed under the GWR main line to access their yard at Kings Meadow.   *Hugh Davies*

both ends, so inconvenient shifts and overtime were never going to cramp my style!"

"Link 3, of a lesser size, was known as 'The Old Man's Gang'. As the name implies these were men responsible for all the shed and yard shunting. Either through choice or for health reasons they had been taken off main line duties".

Roger remembers that an important part of Link 2 duties were the Moreton Yard goods turns. These often involved a light engine trip to Didcot, turning on the triangle at Foxhall Junction or, if unlucky, the turntable at 81E and then back to Moreton. The payload at Moreton yard could sometimes comprise 60 – 70 wagons that might require a 'split' at Scours Lane yard or at the 'New' yards opposite West Junction with the remainder terminating at the Southern yard or moving further east. On one occasion this duty required him to fire a real 'outsider' for the job, a 'Spaceship' BR 9F - that turned up, as Roger remembers "quite out of the blue from Feltham!" Far from being overawed by the arrival of one of the most powerful locos

ever built in Britain, this was as Roger put it, "No big deal. I was used to wide fireboxes from my loan work at Nine Elms and as the 9F box was shallower than the larger firebox of a Merchant Navy I had no problems with this loco." Other duties featuring in Link 2 were the 8.30am Moreton Yard – Feltham, the 3.25pm Moreton – Redhill, a return 8.44am Feltham – Reading Scours Lane and a 'premier' fast service leaving Reading South yard at 7.15pm for Feltham. This was known as 'The Biscuit' and originated from Huntley & Palmers private yards. Reading men ran the service to Feltham where it connected with a fast service to Southampton Docks.

Although Roger does not remember any particular 'rough trips' as such, many of them had their uncomfortable moments." "With a light engine on the GW travelling down from Reading to Moreton Yard, this part of the duty could be a bit hairy, particularly with an S15 or a Q1 which were more used to ambling or slogging along at low speeds. When you were hauling a train there was always a degree of stability at the back end of the tender. Travelling fast, light engine, on an S15 with a full tender of coal was a real pain. The tender would oscillate wildly, having a low front meant the coal used to pour down on to the footplate with the crew knee deep in the stuff. Also, the Q1s being 0-6-0s had a nasty tendency to roll at speed and you used to get thrown all over the shop!". On another occasion he recalls his one and only accident. One day when we had returned from Moreton Yard with a goods for Feltham – I can't remember the date or time, but I do remember we had a BR Class 4 2-6-0 – we ran as usual up Reading Spur where we were to come off the train and return to Reading South shed. Waiting in the headshunt was a Maunsell N or U that was due to take the train on to Feltham. After uncoupling, my driver 'thought' he had the signal to take us on to the main line and back to the shed. However, the signal was a 'dummy' as opposed to a 'board'; the driver should have realised the difference but he didn't and the 'dummy' took us straight into the headshunt and a heavy collision with the SR Mogul. The outcome was 'Maunsell 1' – 'Riddles 0' in

that the only damage to the Maunsell was a bent draw bar but the Riddles had both buffers knocked off. If I recall correctly the Feltham fireman also suffered a lacerated ear which required hospital treatment and I would not wish to make light of that."

Roger also refers to 'competing' with the WR services on the four-track section between Reading and Didcot. There were quite a few tales of 'racing days' going back over the years and the pick of these had to be the efforts of Reading South men to pass the up 'Red Dragon' before Reading General to arrive in the South yards before the Paddington-bound service passed by on the embankment above them. A well-known fireman (and later guard) at Reading South, Ray Ruffell, maintains that on a particular Moreton turn while firing to a young passed fireman, Den Eamer with S15 No 30838, they actually passed 'the Dragon' at Cholsey. With clear signals and waved encouragement from the 'bobbies' all the way into Reading they were into the Southern yards before 'The Dragon'

SECR Wainwright Class D 'Coppertop' No 31488 of 1902 vintage awaits her next duty at Reading South shed on 23 April 1955. At the time the loco was allocated to Gillingham (73D) and may well have been fulfilling that shed's duty 225 that was a 'D' duty for the 10.16am Redhill to Reading passenger service. The loco was reallocated to Guildford (70C) in the October and was withdrawn from there in February 1956, the last year that the class saw service. The engine retains the original large circular spectacle window and unlike others of the class was not fitted with both rectangular and circular spectacles. The class were universally popular amongst SR engine crews as being free steamers, robust and generally reliable even when overdue for overhaul.

Hugh Davies

E4 No 32501 in store at the back of the shed. Again the GW main line may be seen on the embankment above.

Hugh Davies

passed them seconds later. Although Roger in his time at Reading South had heard of some of these tales, his view is a more cautious one. "I had heard of deeds of 'derring-do' along the GW main line between Didcot and Reading but they do need to be taken with a pinch of salt. Realistically, a Castle in good nick with nine or ten on is not going to be hard pushed to outpace Ns/Us/Q1s/S15s/or a BR 4 or 5 slogging along with 60 loose-coupled, unbraked goods wagons. It is true that once you got going, had the road and perhaps the benefit of a fitted train you could crack on a bit on this stretch but given even odds you were never going to see off a fast passenger. There was also the problem of stopping. 800 tons trundling along at 55mph with only the engine and guard's van for braking tended to lead to a serious case of 'discretion before valour'. Perhaps there were a few isolated examples like the one related by Ray but these would be dependent on the coincidence of friendly 'bobbies', the WR service perhaps delayed en-route by signal checks and as long as the composition of the Southern train was of a fully 'fitted' nature." Roger admits that one of the older driving legends at Reading South, one Tom Flight (of appropriate surname), was remembered for his exploits on the GW main line. "Without doubt some drivers were faster than others and one of these was Tom Flight who had a reputation with the GW signalmen for 'getting a move on' with the Moreton services. He revelled in his

nickname of "Mainline". This was given to him as a result of him regularly shouting a hopeful "Main Line" up to the 'bobbies' at Reading Southern and East Main (and probably their equivalents at Didcot) in order to be routed along the main line thus avoiding the delays experienced along the relief lines. Sometimes it worked, sometimes it didn't."

Appropriately enough, Tom Flight was present on the very last day of steam working from Reading to Redhill - 1 January 1965, in charge of U No 31627. That week had seen no less than 10 different N and U locos performing on the services, ousting many of the BR 2-6-0s and 2-6-4Ts that had taken over many of the turns. In a dramatic swan-song Us Nos 31627, 31790/91/99, 31800/09 and Ns 31405/08, 31816/31/58/62 were all seen at Reading.

In recalling the diversity that was the spice of life at the depot, Roger remembers with a certain amount of chagrin that in an age of 'perks', official or otherwise, he never profited from any. "Not even the regular Tuesday hand-outs of Huntley & Palmer broken biscuits and faulty cakes. I also recall that on the early or late passenger turns (i.e. when it was dark) we would stop at one of the manned level crossings between Shalford and Dorking and the driver would fill a wheelbarrow with coal and accept a package in return, perhaps some eggs or maybe a chicken. This arrangement was always kept firmly between the driver and the crossing keeper, no perks for me."

'A ROSE AMIDST THE THORNS'

Roger also knew a character whose official name was Jack. Jack was known as 'Holy Joe' or 'Bible Puncher' because he was a regular church-goer. Jack was a former Reading South driver and destined to become the last shed foreman. He was a stickler for detail, although to be fair what he didn't know about the railway operation really wasn't worth knowing. Reading South was very much a location that was left to get on with things with the minimum of interference from 'upstairs' so long as duties were performed efficiently and the services ran to time. However, although Jack was in many ways the epitome of a thorough perfectionist, Roger thinks he often turned a blind-eye to many of the harum-scarum activities that went on around the fringes of depot life as long as these did not interfere with the smooth running of the depot's responsibilities. Roger is also convinced that Jack was well aware of some of the lively off-duty drinking sessions that took place in several of the town's hostelries known for their railway support. Of these, the nearest and probably the most popular for Reading South footplatemen was 'The Rising Sun', literally a stone's throw from the shed and just around the corner from the police station. Roger can recall quite a few 'after hours' sessions there when sometimes there were as many members of the local constabulary present as there were locomen. History is silent as to whether any disciplinary action needed to be taken against locomen found the worse for wear and on duty.

In recalling many other Reading South characters of that time, some of their nicknames remain fixed in his memory. Fireman Derek 'Dickie' Bird, Driver Bill 'Enos' Kirk (the nickname for Bill was a bit more involved: Eno's was an indigestion product of the time. As Bill was known to be a bit of a 'know it all' - hence 'He Knows' - it took very little to convert in homonym style to ENOS!), Driver George 'Foxy' Powell and shed labourers Dan 'The Coalman' (I forget his surname) and 'Buck' Rogers (ditto his Christian name). Other names that come to mind are Driver Geoff Saunders, Firemen Ted Carter, Rupert Ings and Ted New and shed labourer Arthur Ward. Also, and probably unique was Joe Cassar, from Malta who must have been the sole representative from that island to become a fireman on BR."

"George Powell was specially picked by Jack Hewitt to drive a spruced up 'N' No 31831 on the LCGB Maunsell Tour special that ran on 3 January 1965, the last 'official day of steam working from Reading South station. The return leg was behind another 'bulled-up' loco, this time Maunsell Q No 30545 0-6-0, again driven by George".

Mention of the shed labourers reminds Roger of the harsh working practices of the time. "Looking back with the benefit of hindsight, the physicality of it all was beyond comprehension, not so much on the footplate, but that which was required of the shed artisans. Coaling at Reading South was 100% manual despite so-called improvements in the 1940s. I remember Dan 'The Coalman' and 'Buck' Rogers who would off-load coal wagons by the shovel on one side

S15 No 30508 in charge of a lengthy freight about to depart Reading South, April 1955.   *Hugh Davies*

of the coaling bay and then into loco tenders on the other side. The high-sided tenders must have been soul destroying for them, but then others would say that they didn't know any different. In similar vein were the yard labourers who would empty the pits of loco ash to ground level and then load that same ash into a wagon. I think I had an easy life by comparison."

Towards the end of his brief railway career Roger remembers very little of those last days at Reading South. The shed officially closed on 6 April 1964 although it would see a continuation of work beyond the end of steam on the Redhill services. The very last recorded steam visit to the shed appears to be that of N No 31866 on 21August 1965, while the last (unconfirmed) steam appearance along the route itself was by BR Class 4 No 76031 on a Blisworth to Redhill parcels working in December 1966.

"I can remember the stage where we would sign on at the WR shed (by then Reading South had passed to WR jurisdiction) and then we would be required to make our way over to 'our' shed to start work. Although there was an 'official' walking route of about 20 minutes, on one occasion I gave my driver a lift on my motorbike. He said afterwards that he would rather be in charge of a runaway unbraked goods train down Pinks Hill into Guildford than be my passenger again. With the closure of the shed, I know most Southern men

WR 2-6-0 No 6309 leaving Reading South with the 6.50 am to Redhill sometime in 1964. For many years this was a regular WR engine turn and usually featured an engine of either the 43xx (63xx) or 78xx type.   *B K Snow*

went to the WR with others moving on to Basingstoke. A small number, like Geoff Saunders, went over as electric drivers 'on the juice'. At the finish I managed to obtain an almost permanent loan to Nine Elms and after a while at this I then left the railway to pursue my Merchant Navy ambitions".

"I was never attracted by the cleaner but clinical life that diesels offered. In my opinion the comradeship of the steam footplate could never be replaced by the sterility of new age modernity. I can never forget the experiences of 'getting the job done', especially with an ailing loco that had to be coaxed along with a mixture of guile and bloody-mindedness. This required the sort of 'team effort' probably not recognised by today's so-called quality management methods. Graft and skill was the footplate life, with a huge bucket-full of common sense to keep the whole thing

greased and moving"

So ended Roger Latch's railway interlude. Not surprisingly, however, he remains bonded to the steam railway and now finds time to get his hands dirty on the Watercress Line in Hampshire. Here he has renewed acquaintance with at least one of the erstwhile members of Reading South, 'U-boat' No 31806.

Of the shed and station nothing now remains. The shed buildings were demolished by December 1965 and by 1975 the site would be occupied by the Metal Box HQ. The various yards lingered on until the early 1970s when they too disappeared forever apart from a couple of electrified sidings retained for EMU stabling. The station buildings survived for a while as a garage but the site now lies underneath the vast Apex Plaza completed in the late 1980s.

We don't know who, when, where or where - although definitely an original Pacific. Somehow it seemed to fit rather well with the preceding article.

A London-bound express enters Farningham Road in August 1956.

H. C. Casserley.

FARNINGHAM ROAD
A STATION IN KENT

John Woodhead

(Continued from SW20)

Apart from passengers, the potential of the station at Farningham Road was quickly recognised by one Robert George Parker, known more simply as George Parker, a contemporary entrepreneur who had identified the possibilities of Farningham Road as a base for his business. Parker had been attracted to the area by a friend who was a porter at the station. His first business enterprise was that of a coke and coal merchant: the business was reported as operating at the station by 1862. Shortly after this he had expanded as the agent for the Royal Insurance Company. Early ledgers, dating from January 1867, indicate that local people from around the South Darenth, Sutton at Hone and Horton Kirby area, (as well as from Longfield and Swanley and even Leeds), used the office at the station for their insurance requirements.

George Parker was clearly an opportunist - nowadays we would refer to him as an entrepreneur - for he also represented the Faversham brewers, Shepherd Neame, and distributed the company's products from the station. The brewer's own archive refers to a letter sent in April 1871 to George Parker, the newly appointed agent at Farningham Road station. "We will provide a store and allow you the use of it for a nominal consideration, say a penny a week. We must, however, require you to keep a book containing the names of all customers for beer in order that in the event of determination of the agency by death or otherwise we may be able to trace the empty casks. The question of stores is now before the LCDR and until we can contain them, we must make the best arrangements we can for supplying you. We will send a few casks at a time."

Ann English, George Parker's great-grand daughter, recalls that, decades later in the early 1940s, Shepherd Neame deliveries would still arrive in the goods shed, at the London end of the platform. Here the barrels would then be unloaded on to a platform. The beer and wine would then be stored under this platform, in a cellar within the shed, until required by local customers. Records point to many local people buying beer and wine from George Parker, particularly during the period leading up to Christmas. Casks of beer were also bought by farmers to supply those working in the fields during harvest time. Parker's eventually ceased representing Shepherd Neame at some time around 1950.

George was also a representative of the London Manure Company, (there was at one time, a manure shed at Farningham Road). In addition he was agent for 'John Corbett's Worcestershire Salt'. After this length of time it is perhaps slightly puzzling as to why there were sales of Worcestershire Salt in the area, recorded in particular, to the local vicar. More easy to explain is that several local farms took salt in large quantities because this was required for the glebe when the hay was cut; salt would sweeten the hay if put amongst the crop.

The coal merchant's business was very much a family concern, George Parker later passing it on to Henry Edwin Parker and he in turn left it to Harold Edwin Parker. At some stage there was a change of ownership of the business, with a takeover by the Seaborne Coal Company, followed by William Hayman of Rochester. Henry Edwin Parker was employed as manager and in 1947 it returned once more to family ownership until 1956. At its height the Parker business extended to five local coal depots, including one at Eynsford and another at Swanley Junction.

Notwithstanding its position on the main line, Farningham Road had its share of characters amongst the local staff. These included, during the 1940s, Jack Burton the porter who would supplement his meagre railway income by repairing cane-work chairs.

Ann English, a descendent of the Parker dynasty recalls:

"In the booking office, Mr Longley was the station master; he was followed by Mr Tom Hadrill. The latter lived in the station master's house and kept chickens on the other side of the station, where he also had an allotment. When war broke out and the men went off to fight, Nellie Mullinder became the clerk and Mrs Chilmaid was porter. After the war Nellie Mullinder

George Parker

The yard approach, office and coach body.

transferred to be clerk in my father's (coal) office. In the late 1940s, on the wharf, (as the coal yard was called), there was Mrs Callister who could throw a hundred-weight of coal up onto the back of a lorry with the best of them. A supervisor, Mr West, would regularly visit the station. I think he came down from Swanley about once a week to check all the things coming in and going out. His mother, Rose, was one of the last people to be insured through Royal Insurance at the station. Other names recalled were Mrs Churchill, Mrs Harper and one of her sons, and the Goodings, Tom and Titch. The foreman at that time was Harry Wolf. Later I remember there were Alf and George James.

"I have memories of hearing the shunting going on in the goods yard whilst lying in bed as a small child. Some notable trains went through Farningham Road station too: the Royal Train, the Golden Arrow, and, most historic of all, trains packed with exhausted troops, many in tatters, rescued from the Dunkirk beaches.

"There was a wooden crane in the goods shed that was used for unloading deliveries that couldn't be lifted by hand. It was a curio, but a working curio nonetheless. The ganger and his men would regularly cut scrub from the lineside to reduce the risk of sparks from the steam locomotives causing it to catch alight. Even so several fields of crops would regularly catch fire.

"Another thing that Parker's was involved in was as carriers for the Southern Railway, dealing with parcels. Ron Newing worked for my father driving the vehicle that delivered the items that would arrive at the station."

PARKER'S COAL YARD

The coal yard had its own sidings that went as far as the bridge over the Dartford road. The platforms at the station were originally shorter and there were points at the South Darenth end of the station where coal trucks would be manoeuvred into the sidings. Until 1956 wagons of coal would be hand-shunted on the wharf sidings and Ann recalls on quiet Sunday mornings, as a child, she would be allowed to change the points over.

Every letter that was sent by Parker's was copied into a ledger and incoming mail retained. These still survive and include such gems as one from the Goods Manager's Office of the LCDR at Victoria in May 1878 allowing George Parker to 'use a piece of ground 100 feet from the face of the buffer stops and 20 feet from the outside rail of siding next to the main line for the sum of £10 per annum'.

"The coal yard had its four stables for the horses that pulled the coal carts around the area.

"Until as recently as 1998 there was an old LCDR, five-compartment, 3rd class carriage, on the right hand side after entering the yard. One section of this vehicle was the coal sack store, whilst that closest to the station was known as the "men's lobby". Here they had a stove and in wet weather the men would sit, playing cards, and get paid for it!

GEORGE PARKER,
COAL + & + COKE + MERCHANT
Farningham Road Station, L. C. & D. Ry.,
Sutton-at-Hone, Near Dartford.

DEPOTS AT FARNINGHAM ROAD, SWANLEY, AND EYNSFORD.

TRUCK LOADS TO ANY STATION.

*Agent for Messrs. Shepherd, Neame, & Co.'s Faversham Ales ; for
London Manure Co. ; and the Royal Insurance Co.*

WORCESTERSHIRE SALT.

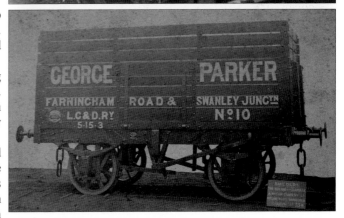

The coal yard office had a wind-up 'candlestick' telephone with the number Farningham 61: the station was Farningham 45."

Theft of coal from the yard at Farningham Road was a constant problem. Ann English explained there were all sorts of ways people would try to get coal illegally.

"They would climb up the embankment and get in through the wire fence to take coal out of the trucks. Norman Bell, the village policeman, would spend nights in the trucks trying to catch the culprits.

"On Saturday mornings our men would go on 'the trolley round', as it was known. This was a circuit of the villages where the people would come out and buy from the lorry. If an elderly customer was unable to carry his (or her) coal there'd always be a little boy with a pram who would wheel it back for them."

Harold Parker, using his experience as a horticulturist, planted out the slogan 'Coal for Comfort' on a piece of ground next to the yard entrance.

The yard passed out of Parker family ownership sometime around 1956 and was sold to G. Hughes. Sometime after 1961 the original offices at the coal yard burnt down.

By the early 1960s the coal yard was no longer being supplied with rail deliveries, with road transport taking over. This would not have been permitted earlier for a clause in Parker's contract prohibited the supply of coal other than by the railway.

Apart from on the main line, trains to Gravesend would call, often having started at St Mary Cray. The service was limited to three morning and two evening trains and as such catered mainly for workmen and schoolchildren. On Saturday the service encouraged a little more travel with ten trains. Many people in the Farningham Road area would use these trains to visit Gravesend for shopping or recreation.

Tony Carter in his book *'To The Railway Born'* recalls his own time serving at Farningham Road.

"In 1964 I was promoted to station master at Farningham Road, between Swanley and Rochester. When I went there I was surprised to find the goods yard still in use, as many had closed by then. We were still receiving coal and a few other 'full loads' and it was rumoured that a large steel

Top - Staff of H. E. Parker stand beside the last truck to deliver coal to the firm in 1956.

Centre - The former LCDR 5-compartment 3rd class carriage which served as a mess room and coal stack store.

Bottom - Private owner wagon from the Midland Railway Carriage & Wagon Co.

Looking towards London in 1921during work to raise the level of the platforms.

works was to be erected there on the many acres of spare land which were available on the 'up' side. Here could be seen several sidings long since abandoned and now overgrown. (The steel works were opened a few years later and for a while had rail access).

"Farningham Road box was switched in when a freight went in or out of the yard or a train was being sent down the single goods line to Gravesend West. The box had a small panel which operated the junction where previously Fawkham Junction box had been. This branch was operated as 'one man working' with a 'dead' staff with a key on the end for intermediate sidings; the staff was not issued from a tablet machine at Farningham Road. The main-line signalling was 'track circuit block' and the signals were semi-automatic, in other words when Farningham Road switched out, the signals returned to automatic working.

"The main line through Farningham Road was a renowned spot for fast running and before I came and after I left there were several derailments of freight trains there, train-ferry wagons usually being responsible. It was said that several fruit trees had grown up along the line as a result of fruit spilled when a wagon turned over! I am reminded of the time when a 'ferry van' arrived at Farningham Road from the continent for a local consignee and our attention was drawn to an important notice on the

outside of the van in a foreign language which, of course, we did not understand. Without further ado we opened the wagon door and were bombarded with loose oranges.

"Farningham Road presented problems with ticket checks as it had a footbridge away from the station buildings and it was impossible for a man to cover both.

"The station house which we occupied was small and compact, unlike most, but the only piece of garden was on the other side of the track and when I had a bonfire there one afternoon I almost burned down the signal box!

"The house and signal box were lit by electricity but the station was gas lit. Farningham Road was a typical Chatham & Dover Railway station with very tiny buildings on one end of the platform. There was no structure on the down side except the underneath of an old water crane which served as a waiting room.'

Further memories come from Brian Grant in his 1998 book *'Home and Distant'*, including three derailments in the vicinity of Farningham Road.

"The first derailment involved a train of 'vanfits' on the down line at Farningham Road. One of the wagons had suffered a fractured wheelset, causing a number of wagons to be derailed and serious damage to about a mile of track. On arrival at the site we examined the derailed wagons and found the fractured wheelset by the side of the track but could not find the wagon to which it belonged. Eventually, after quite a long search, we spotted it lying in the garden of a bungalow some 50 feet below the railway. Descending the embankment to assess the damage, we spoke to the owner who said that she was hanging out the washing when she heard a loud noise and, on looking up, saw the wagon literally flying through the air. She then went indoors and telephoned her husband to say, 'It has happened.' It appears that the couple had been expecting just such an incident ever since they arrived at the bungalow.

"The second incident at Farningham Road was on the up line and involved a train of wagons loaded with fruit and vegetables. In this incident a number of wagons were derailed causing the coupling between the first and second wagon to break. When we arrived at the scene we found the area literally covered in crushed fruit and vegetables.

"In later years refuse from the Camberwell area of London was loaded into mineral wagons at the Elephant & Castle sidings, which were then conveyed to a refuse tip near Farningham Road. On arrival at site the locomotive propelled the wagons into refuge sidings from whence they were moved by tractor to the point of discharge. On one occasion a raft of wagons ran away and became derailed at the end of a siding where there were no buffer stops. As can be imagined, the ground in a refuse tip is not firm enough to allow the use of a crane or jacks and packing, so it was decided to try to haul the wagons back towards the main line where the ground was much firmer. Some of the nearer wagons were recovered successfully, but during attempts to recover the last two a chain broke and the broken link just missed a member of the breakdown crew. In the end it was deemed safer to leave these two wagons to be broken up for scrap."

Other memories, this time of a train-spotter in the area between 1949 and 1952 appeared in STEAM WORLD in October and November 1999 penned by John Skinner and David Leggett.

Memories of a signalman

Harry Barrett was a Signalman at Farningham Road from 1956 to 1965. His working life on the railways began in 1946 at Orpington as a Junior Porter and then Signal Lad. He then went into the army after which he spent two years working at Eynsford Station, then Chelsfield before coming to Farningham Road. He retired from Dartford in 1996. As an account of his life on the railway, it is recalled by him with obvious warmth and genuine affection for the people he worked with:

"I passed out for Signalman in autumn 1956, a job I always found very interesting. We seemed to have quite a bit of freight traffic going through Farningham Road. The stationmaster was called Wally Sinden and was a churchgoer who attended the Baptist Chapel at Sutton at Hone. I can

truthfully say that I never heard him swear, although he must have come close to it at times with the staff. He always used to call everybody "Old Man" or "Old Chap", so all the staff used to take the mickey and call each other "Old Man" or "Old Chap"- but only when Wally wasn't about!

A good mate to be on with was Norman Featherstone whom I had seen round at Eynsford. He was a relief porter but was at Farningham Road for some years. Don Allen was one of the signalmen there, and also relief signalman was Harry Smith, who used to talk very slowly; so everyone would pull his leg. George Gooding, who lived in New Road, was the shunter. He was good at fly shunting with coal wagons and traffic from Horton Kirby Paper Mill. Fly shunting was when the shunter and goods guard detached coal and Horton Kirby Paper Mill traffic, (china clay, coal and gypsum), from the engine and the hand brakes on the wagons were released and the shunter would use a brake stick or shunting pole. The engine gave a nudge to the wagons and the guard would also assist this movement and slowly the wagons were placed in position in the sidings. This was a skill that required absolute control of the movement and allowed the engine to go into another part of the sidings.

"On one occasion whilst fly shunting, George found himself on his own with no goods guard to help him brake the wagons. A line of trucks came down No 1 sidings, hit the stops and caused three wagons of Horton Kirby Paper Mill coal wagons to derail. It didn't affect the main line, but the impact was enough to knock off all the ornaments on the mantelshelf in the stationmaster's front room and caused the gas lamps to have their lights knocked out on the platforms."

"The goods porter, 'Slim' Whitman, was responsible for sheeting wagons of material sent up by HKPM and used to send machinery away from Garrett & Sons, who dealt with farm machinery. We also received

Photograph from the 1950s by John Refford, including the goods shed and stationmasters house.

The 2.27 to Gravesend leaves Farningham Road in April 1938.

farm machinery that was unloaded on the dock road – No 2 siding: his was also the goods shed road. The dock was used to load and unload cattle and machinery. the goods shed to load and unload crated traffic.

"Fred Taylor was the booking clerk, who lived with his wife and family at Farningham Home for Boys, where Mrs Taylor was a house mother. Fred was a bit slow on occasions and once let three or four calves roam from the booking hall on to the track. Fortunately there weren't any trains about, and luckily the calves never touched the live rail and we somehow managed to get them off the track.

"Jack Burton was the late turn porter. I had met him originally at Eynsford where he was relief porter. He looked about 80 then but was probably only about 65. I recall he always looked old and was also a crafty old devil.

"The permanent way gang were Bill Hammond, ganger; George Parker, sub-ganger; and platelayers Charlie Case, George Rogers and Bill Rogers, the last two named being cousins. They would all come to the box for a cup of tea when they were working nearby.

"George Gooding, the shunter, could always be found fiddling with his car when he wasn't shunting. One day he dug a trench in the old ARP sidings so that he could change the engine oil. A few days later on the Saturday evening the stationmaster was walking round the sidings and fell into this hole which was covered in leaves and chalk stains. I was sitting in the box and suddenly heard footsteps on the troughing near the cabin and a voice saying, "I say old chap, who dug a hole in the siding?" When I looked out

of the window, it just amused me and I had to laugh, but Wally Sinden wasn't so happy and said, "It's nothing to laugh at, old chap" – all without swearing! When I next saw George Gooding I told him what had happened and that I had told the stationmaster that I didn't know who had dug the hole. George hadn't any sympathy for Wally and said that it served him right for snooping around the sidings.

"George was shunting one night in the sidings. I wasn't on duty at the time and Harry Smith was the signalman. It had started to pour down with rain, just as George had finished the shunting, and as he walked on the cable troughing near the signal box, he slipped and landed up to his armpits in the place where we used to throw our tealeaves. Needless to say, it wasn't very pleasant and George struggled up the signal box steps and kicked at the door to be let in. But Harry Smith had locked the door and told George to clear off and to go down to the porter's room and wash and clean himself up and then he would let him in.

"A few days later a spare coupling had been left in the down sidings, so I nipped over the line and put this coupling in the back of George's car. He took it backwards and forwards between his home in New Road and the station for days before he found it.

"The mill drivers used to unload the clay traffic and fuel that was used in the Horton Kirby Paper Mill and they would sometimes come up to the box when they had unloaded the wagons. It was a busy station, the clay traffic for Horton Kirby Paper Mill was very steady and we would have about four or five wagons daily, Monday to Friday.

"One evening I asked one of the engine drivers if he would give me a lift to St. Mary Cray but he said that he would take me as far as Swanley and drop me off there as the adverse gradient at St. Mary Cray meant that it would be a job to get going again. I accepted and was asked if I would care to fire the engine, I agreed, so I got on and the fireman gave me the shovel. My first three or four attempts weren't very successful but after a while I started to get the hang of it and the driver and fireman said I'd done quite well.

"When I was dropped off at Swanley I noticed that people on the platform kept looking at me and it wasn't until I looked in a mirror in the carriage that I saw that my face was covered in coal dust. I didn't ask for any more lifts after that.

"Around the end of 1957, colour-light signalling was being brought in on the Victoria to Chatham and Gillingham line, with the addition that the signal boxes from Farningham Road to Sole Street could be switched out of circuit on occasions. We signalmen would then be expected to assist on the platform and in the goods yard as required.

"When the colour-light signalling was installed, Farningham was given control of the Gravesend West line. A key token machine was installed and a token was taken out of the machine when a particular track circuit became operative. The key was put in the pouch and the driver/fireman was given the key which allowed him on to the single line at Fawkham Junction to go on to Gravesend West. One day the train coming down from Hither Green approached the platform at Farningham too fast. I was standing on the approach to the down platform, ready to give them the key, but he passed by too quickly to be able to hand it over. The train had to stop and the fireman had to run back to me for it.

"Jack Burton, the leading porter on late turn, used to do chimney-sweeping in his spare time and often came off the early train with his soot bag, sweeping rods and his clean uniform in a bag. I saw him come off one day at about 10:00 a.m. for a sweeping job in Sutton at Hone. I gather that he had problems with his rods which got stuck up the chimney and he and his lady customer were shoving and pulling the rods when, all of a sudden, the brush and rods came down the chimney and covered the pair of them, (and the lady's front room), in about a ton of soot. The news got back to the station and old Jack had his leg pulled for a long time after this.

"Another Jack Burton adventure was with an Alsatian dog that Jack had collected off a down train and took over the crossing boards to the booking office, where he phoned the dog's new master. Before he did this, Jack took off the dog's muzzle and gave it a drink, but while Jack had his back turned, talking on the phone, the dog wolfed down Jack's sandwiches. Jack told the dog's master about this, hoping to be compensated, but the chap wouldn't give Jack anything and told Jack he shouldn't have taken the muzzle off.

"A couple of hours later, the chap came back with the dog and asked Jack to send it back, but Jack said that he couldn't do that because the kennels would be closed and that he wasn't allowed to leave animals unattended in the booking office and that the owner would have to bring it back on Monday for it to be sent. Monday came round and the dog was sent off and put in with the guard. Evidently the muzzle hadn't been put on properly and the train guard finished up standing on his desk when the dog went berserk and the RSPCA had to be sent for at Bromley South.

"Jack was always on the scrounge and one day he had gone into the yard to look into a railway van wagon for seed spuds: the local farmers used to get them delivered by rail and there was always a fair amount left over. So Jack was up in the van with a sack when somebody thought they would have a bit of fun and shut him in! I wasn't on duty at the time, but apparently Wally Sinden was walking round the yard and heard Jack banging and shouting and let him out. He could have finished up at Hither Green.

"I was on early turn one day when a woman came up to the station to see if we could weigh her dog, a great dane. It was very big and very playful. It stood up and put its paws on Norman's shoulders and was taller than Norman, who was at least six foot five. We tried to weigh the dog on the booking office scales but he wouldn't stand still so we thought we would try the scales in the goods shed which were bigger but it still wasn't any good as the dog just kept jumping about all over the place, so we had to give it up as a bad job. At least the lady owner appreciated our efforts.

"Sometimes we sent pigs by rail on a passenger train and never had any bother sending them in their crates, but one day we had a pig come in a crate and we spent nearly ten minutes trying to get it in a passenger train, but the crate was too big so had to be sent on a van train.

"The Railway had a contract to send about six churns of milk a day from Farningham to the Bourne and Hillier milk depot at Chatham and nearly every time we moved them we would get soaked in milk when it came over the top, so we used to try to catch each other out sometimes with the churns when we tipped them.

"I was on duty one night when I heard a few bangs in the early hours of the morning, but thought that they were only crow-scarers going off. At about 3:20 a.m. I heard someone on the troughing outside the box. I looked out and there was a chap, about 30 years-old standing there. I asked him what he wanted and he said that he wanted to get to Fawkham Station. I told him the first train was at 5:40 a.m. He seemed to know about the paper train which came through at 3:40. I told him it didn't stop here. He said he would walk along the track but I said he couldn't as it was too dangerous. He could trip and land on the live rail. I felt sorry for him and so I unlocked the door and invited him in. He said he would just go down and pick up his gun. I didn't think much about this at the time. I gave him a cup of tea and a biscuit and we had a smoke and a chat. When the

Herne Hill goods was due at 4:45 a.m. I said he could go onto the down platform now as I had work to do.

"When the goods train came in, Bert Reeves the guard asked me why that chap had come down from the box. He recognised him from hanging around Fawkham Station several times. The chap eventually caught the first train down and I forgot all about him. At about 6:15 a.m. I was offered the first passenger train to London and I rang to offer the train to Swanley. Swanley accepted and as I started to pull the signals off, I looked at number 6 Up Advance signal and saw it come off to a white light. I then realised that the chap I'd had in the box had been taking pot shots at the signals and had blown the green glass out. Needless to say, we never saw him again.

"Don Allen left in 1962 and George Chandler, a signal lad from Swanley, came down to take Don's job. I think he found the work a bit hard. We used to have to fold truck sheets used by Horton Kirby Paper Mills in papermaking. It was a messy old job to fold them, especially on a windy day, and we generally left them until a calmer day. But George wanted to do it straightaway. Norman had hold of one rope and George the other, when suddenly a gust of wind took the rope out of Norman's hand and the sheet wrapped itself around George. He had great difficulty in unwrapping himself and was swearing like a trooper, when, rather unfortunately, the Vicar of Darenth came onto the platform. George was very ashamed of himself, but the Vicar just caught his train and didn't say anything to anybody.

"When Arthur Matthews became stationmaster he had the idea of cleaning the truck sheets using the old cattle pens and the hoses. The sheets were often covered in clay or lime. Word got out that Farningham Road were cleaning truck sheets and so goods yards up and down the line began sending their dirty sheets for cleaning. The scheme didn't last more than three or four weeks after that.

"During the summer of 1961 someone threw a metal bucket on the line from the Farningham Boys Bridge that welded itself to the electric running rail on the down line. The end shoe beam of a Victoria to Ramsgate train caught the whole lot up and caused track circuits in the signal box to show a fault on the line. I immediately brought the signal box into circuit and blocked the line by giving the 'obstruction danger' bell signal. The down line was out of action for about five days and there was an inquiry a week later in London and I had to go to explain what had happened and the reason for the action I took.

"The gas lamps on the station were relics from a bygone age and they were maintained by an infrequent gas fitter who came down from London. His shed was on the down platform next to the down side waiting room. There were about eight lamps on the down side, twelve on the up side and four on the bridge.

"Sometimes, on a Sunday, Les Thompson, who used to live in Shrubbery Road, would bring some of his homing pigeons up in wicker baskets to be sent off on the train; most went to Orpington. They were put in with the

On 1 August 1953, the last day of the passenger service on the Gravesend West branch, No 31671 waits to take the 3.04 service to Gravesend.

A London bound 'Bulleid' in 1956, with a pair of trucks in the sidings.

guard. Old Jack Burton, the late turn porter, would deal with these but he couldn't spell 'pigeons' and always put 'pie gons' on the waybill.

"In the early 1960s, the time Arthur Matthews was station master, he would get very annoyed by early morning passengers using the window sills of his back room, which overlooked the up platforms, as benches. He was also very upset one morning when he came to unlock the booking office to be confronted by a herd of sheep. The story goes that they had been delivered late one evening and the only way through to the lorry that was to transport them away from the station was through the booking hall. Having herded them from the platform into the building, however, staff discovered that the outside door was locked and it was decided to leave the animals there until the morning. Arthur was met with an unpleasant smell and a lot of mess!"

John Woodhead has produced privately the story of Farningham Road station. Copies are available at £6.00 + £2.00 postage. John may be contacted at: johnwoodhead@hotmail.co.uk

Undated aerial view.

'THE PERKS OF THE JOB'

(...and the early Railtours of the 'REC')

Ron Mason

The Railway Enthusiasts Club (REC) based at Farnborough was unique having a clubroom that enabled much socialising amongst enthusiasts some of whom were railway staff and ingenious ideas were often conjured up there to further their interests.

Before Dr. Beeching closed many rural branch lines and stations coupled with the withdrawal of steam locos, many enthusiasts transferred their attention from train spotting to travelling on as many lines as possible on the railway map. Some of these individuals travelled on the many Rail Tours organised over normally non passenger routes by societies, whilst enthusiasts who also worked for the railway had a useful tool in that a perk of the job allowed not only reduced rate fares but also a number of free passes each year. These could have been made out between any two stations of their choosing. The latter had to be applied for from the staff office by completing an application form, simply noting the two stations between which the applicant wanted to travel. There was no geographical or time limit to using these passes and a simple blank card ticket was issued with the two stations writtten in by hand. This gave the opportunity not only to cover a wide area but because ticket collectors (some knowing the score) rarely if ever clipped these tickets either at the station or on the train, they might be used for several journeys over and above the official 'once only out and back' limit.

Some cunning individuals were quick to realise that to gain best use of this facility, small wayside stations would be best designated as the destination as these would possibly confuse or be ignored by ticket collectors not totally familiar with the entire railway network. Sometimes enthusiasts would deliberately stretch the concession by jokingly applying station names that caused obvious amusement. Examples were Three Cocks to Four Oaks via Sevenoaks, and Newport to Newport via Newport. On one occasion a ticket collector, probably accepting the joke, looked at the ticket of an enthusiast going through a barrier at York. The ticket was made out St. Erth to Georgemas Junction. The collector looked at it, turned it upside down and turned to the passenger and said, "Well I hope you know where you're bloody well going cause I am damned if I do" In effect this one ticket gave the holder almost complete coverage of the entire network from Cornwall to the north of Scotland!

One of the most amusing stories told related to certain unadvertised workmens' special trains and other special service routes. An application was sent in for a ticket from Weymouth Quay (used for boat trains) to Barrow Shipyard (a branch used by dockyard staff). The application was sent back saying that nobody could find any boats that

Unfortunately it has been impossible to locate any images of 'The Hampshire Hog' so instead we show an REC outing of 15 October 1960 when M7 No 30028 was utilised on the 'North Hampshire'. This commenced at Farnborough, thence Aldershot Government Sidings-Bordon-Alton -Treloar's Siding-Farringdon- Frimley and return to Farnborough. The special is seen here at Frimley almost at the end of its journey.

Roger Holmes

covered this route (bearing in mind that the railways also ran some boat services) and it took some convincing of the staff personnel before the ticket was agreed.

Continuing on with the theme of the tours organised by the REC, the club's organizing committee decided to arrange a tour in 1964 to cover lines in Hampshire and adjacent areas, some of which were not normally covered by passenger services. It was also always a tradition to give each tour a name (following on from some of the more famous names like the 'Flying Scotsman' and the 'Royal Scot' etc). In this case, as the tour centred around Guildford, as such it was thought what could be better than using part of the name given to a local geological formation "The Hog's Back": so the name of the train "The Hampshire Hog" was born. Of course most named main line trains carried a headboard on the front of the engine and some REC members decided to make a headboard for this train. One member who had building and artistic skills, got to work designing and building a colourfully painted headboard complete with a hog's head and the name of the train inscribed around the outside. It was unveiled at one of the club meetings to an instant roar of approval and it was felt would add a sense of importance to the train. It was also the norm for a small descriptive booklet to be produced for each passenger on the tour containing the itinerary and some historical details and this too also proudly carried the name of the train.

Shortly after the tour, plans were being discussed and prepared for the next venture. Going further afield, the club looked at the Peterborough area which had a vast array of lines, many of which had been built to serve the large brickworks area. Because the area involved was quite extensive and as the bricks had to be transported from one part to another during the process, from excavation of the raw material, to the moulding, drying and final firing of the bricks, rail transport had been provided at an early stage. Peterborough itself was also an important railway centre and junction, serving several routes and the brickworks added to the number of lines that could be included in a tour, many of which radiated out from the main lines. A tour seemed a must and as plans were being prepared, the need for a suitable name arose. Peterborough, although geographically part of Cambridgeshire, was closely associated with the adjacent Lincolnshire, home of sausages. Inspiration arose amongst the planners and what could be better than in the tradition of the REC using a name to follow on from before. To the further delight of members the name, "The Peterborough Porker" was conjured up, again much to the amusement of the Peterborough locals and the press with much explaining needing to be done to describe some of the clubs activities and the relevance of the name. This elicited further amusement amongst all concerned not least also at the sight of the itinerary booklet some of the passengers were holding inscribed with the heading of the name of the tour.

Sometime later, further tour plans were being made and requests had been received to try and cover a group of lines within the Forest of Dean in Gloucestershire near to the Welsh border. A number of open-cast coal mines had been opened within the area of Coleford and Cinderford many years previously and access to these was made by a line leaving Lydney on the main route from Gloucester to Newport. A tour was planned and after some negotiation with British Railways Western Region permission was given for the tour to run but the train would have to be made up of brake-vans due to restrictions with passenger coaches on some of the lines. The club committee spent much time making preparations for the tour but could not decide on an all important name for the train. Local geological features of the area were considered until at last a stroke of genius (in the true style of the REC's - some would say eccentric - frame of mind) was dreamt up by one of the members. The main line from Gloucester to Newport ran alongside the River Severn and a well known feature associated with the river was the Severn Bore, a massive tidal flow of water which came regularly up the river from the Bristol Channel. Without a moment's further hesitation a name was adopted and the train was named THE SEVERN BOAR after howls of mirth at one of the Committee meetings and later from members. Again an itinerary booklet was printed and distributed with the name of the train emblazoned on the front cover. On the tour day and as was expected by the diehard members and to their further amusement, some mutterings were heard at Lydney station amongst locals who had come to see the train and who had seen a copy of the tour booklet. News of the tour had reached the local news media and television stations who arrived at Lydney to observe. The train had been formed in the goods yard at Gloucester and ran to Lydney to pick up passengers. As it arrived, awaiting passengers were interviewed and when one of the organizers produced a copy of the itinerary booklet with the tour name highlighted a news correspondent quickly explained rather hesitatingly that the name had been spelt wrongly, which was obviously anticipated.

Further amusement amongst the passengers was obvious and the media team suitably embarrassed at not being familiar with the previous club activities. The tour went extremely well at first. It was to be a full day and as the small 0-6-0 tank locomotive used from the start had emptied its bunker of coal by early afternoon, a second loco had been organized to come from Gloucester to take over the train for the rest of the tour. Possibly due to the over-exuberance of the train crew running light engine at speed along the main line to Lydney, smoke was seen coming from an axle box when it arrived for the transfer and it was decided that it definitely could not be used to take over as anticipated. An air of desperation quickly arose amongst passengers and organizers whilst some with railway operating experience thought up a solution to the problem. The second engine obviously had a full bunker of coal which was desperately needed so the two engines were drawn up alongside each other on adjacent tracks in the

Lydney yard with their bunkers next to each other. The crews, the organizers and the enthusiasts then formed a type of chain gang hanging on to various parts of the two engines to transfer the huge pieces of coal from one bunker to the other to the general encouragement and amusement of the rest of the passengers: enthusiasts were well used to improvisation in terms of railway operations.

The tour was eventually restarted with many on board now having blackened hands and faces but at least they knew they would not now miss out some of the lines they were hoping to cover. By late afternoon the train was well behind schedule and on returning to Lydney to travel back up the main line to Gloucester many of the passengers who had travelled from the south via Paddington were becoming concerned that they would not connect with the last train of the day back to London. Fortunately, the local railway operating staff appreciated the problem and on request agreed to hold the last train at Gloucester to await the arrival of our train.

The ultimate scene at Gloucester Station became worthy of a comedy show. Passengers on the London train were becoming exasperated at the unknown (or unexplained) reason for their delayed departure and some had got off the train to try to gain information from any staff they could see on the platform. The main platform at Gloucester station was a long one, easily having room for the London express with room to spare. This meant it would be possible, using calling on signal arrangements, to allow "The Severn Boar" to run into the same platform and draw up behind the London train. A look of dumbstruck horror appeared on the faces of the waiting passengers on the platform who saw this train composed only of brake vans approaching. Climbing down from the brake vans on to the platform came the enthusiasts appearing initially to be normal passengers, some carrying small bags and cases (those who had stayed away the night before the tour), but on closer inspection, their general covering of coal dust caused some concern. Hurriedly, many clambered aboard the London train, and as it departed the tour members settled into their seats. As was to be expected curiosity got the better of certain regular passengers who had been kept waiting. The enthusiasts had prepared for this and tried to keep looking serious with their amusement bottled. "Have you come far?" and "Were you delayed?" came the questions and in rather dulcet tones and with an expression of disdain for the railway generally they replied, "Oh our previous train broke down and we had to travel in guards' vans". The other passengers sat back, at first with an air perhaps of pity rather than disbelief, but then decided to exacerbate the situation by going into further details. Eventually the temptation of the "anoraks" to explain more overcame them especially as they wished to use the return journey to discuss amongst themselves plans for further forthcoming plans which the other passengers would possibly overhear. The full description of the day's events was explained which some found it difficult to believe but eventually by the time the train reached Paddington it had been accepted and a general sense of merriment was shared by all, the term "railway enthusiasm" taking on a whole new meaning.

'The Severn Boar' special deep in the Forest of Dean at Coleford Junction.   *Roger Holmes*

'REBUILT' - THE LETTERS AND COMMENTS PAGES

I will admit to having done it again - little space left. So without further ado….and firstly from Fred Neill of the South Western Circle, "The photo of the collecting dog in issue 22 is <u>probably</u> of John Bovett's third Exeter area publicised dog "Kim", described as a golden retriever. This was his 1950s dog - "Nigger" & "Sandy" the previous two were both black. Strangely, Bovett actually seems to have had a fourth - generally unpublicised dog - "Beaulew Jack" in 1947. (The excellent "Exeter memories" website http://www.exetermemories.co.uk/em/1940s.php has some details on the three including amounts collected.)

Now from Alan Postlethwaite and which is a follow on from some further notes from Richard Bell on Alan's recent article on 'The Battersea Tangle'. "I am grateful to Richard Bell for his additional notes on The Battersea Tangle. I would suggest that there is scope for more detailed articles on railway conglomerations in this area as follows: (a) Stewarts Lane & Longhedge Works (b) Pimlico & Battersea Park MPD and Goods Station and (c) Nine Elms Works and MPDs. I am aware that another author is currently preparing a society paper on Nine Elms Goods Station."

And that, would you believe, is it for now although I will end with a précis of some delightful memories recently from Brian Cox, "My father was the Railway Crossing keeper at Salmon Pool Crossing, Crediton, Devon, and I was born there in January, 1932. During the war, an engine came towards our crossing, frantically sounding off it's whistle. Dad came out to try to find out why the driver was getting so excited, only to realize that the engine was stopping unofficially at our home. The driver handed down a large suit case, saying, " You have an unexpected visitor, and he asked me to hand you this case to save him carrying it from Crediton Station." With a couple of quick blasts on the whistle the train proceeded. As it drew away, it revealed a much loved Uncle, a Royal Naval Officer, standing on the other side of the track, having craftily stayed on the train, only to dismount on the blind side whilst his case was unprofessionally being delivered. Fortunately, railway officialdom was none the wiser.

"Admiring my Uncle, later I also joined the Royal Navy as a boy seaman in 1947. Following my service, including serving as a Submariner, I was discharged into Civvy street, creating the need for civilian employment in late 1957.

"By a series of coincidences, which are another story, I found myself in the office of Mr. Sam Waterman, the West Country Area Manager of the Southern Railway Signal and Telecommunication Department, which resulted in my becoming a temporary labourer within his department on 16 December, 1957, aged 25.

"Having learnt much from my Uncle, and pretending to be ignorant of the ruling that I was not allowed to apply for any promotions published on the frequent vacancy lists until I was made a member of permanent staff, I applied for a list of six vacancies in the London Area home counties. Not being worried by being reprimanded for the error of my ways, I defended myself by claiming that the fault did not lie with me, but with Sam Waterman, as he should have told me of any limitations at the outset.

"In his words, "For your bloody cheek, I will send your six applications through to head office, and let them sort it out." The result was my instant promotion to the post of Assistant Installer at Staines, providing I accepted to undergo training for Assistant Lineman. Hence started an interesting career, which lasted thirty five years, and later saw me retiring from British Rail as a Signal Engineering Manager myself.

"Initially I had been taken on at Exeter Central as a lorry driver, but with other duties within the Telegraph Pole Gang. These other duties consisted mainly of assisting the linemen when the latter were aloft on telegraph poles. Often I was also on one end of a spade digging holes for the replacement of telegraph poles. Other work included drilling rails for the installation of bonding around joints for track circuiting, and many other types of work of an electrical nature. Hence, we as a gang became involved with more and more major projects such as the re-modeling of the Weymouth Layout and new Signal Box.

"It was on these more major projects, and other work throughout the vast West of England district, which were frequently at considerable distances from our home depot, that it was necessary to sleep over in close proximity to the work site. Often this could be to sleep in conveniently berthed carriage stock, but with this, there was always the hazard of finding yourself being transported miles away by the unexpected repositioning of your mobile sleeping arrangements.

"I guess that having been a sailor, I was fully capable of adapting my nautical experiences to cope with the lesser hardships and difficulties of my new railway environment, and as I still had my hammock from my Naval days, it was a simple matter to improve my sleeping arrangements within our gang's Mess & Tool Van. I soon realized that by removing the existing bolts from conveniently spaced roof beams and replacing them with extended eye bolts, I could easily restore or maintain the structural integrity of the van's roof support, whilst also providing suitable anchor points to allow me to sling my hammock from them. A centrally positioned third eyebolt also allowed me to hoist my hammock up tight to the van roof conveniently clear of causing any obstruction when not in use for sleeping.

"I also stowed away a primus stove, a frying pan, a pressure cooker, together with a plate and eating irons in a locker. On each day, especially on those weekend days away, I took ready prepared food in Kilner Jars and other sealed containers, such that I could quickly and easily prepare myself a hot meal with a minimum of fuss. There was also a coal fired stove built into the van, so this could also be used, not only for warmth, but to brew up tea, heat pies etc., so much so, that my initiatives were to become the envy of my workmates, in that I was able to provide so well for myself.

"When progressing from one work site to another, arrangements were made with the shunters to include our van on a convenient goods train. It was also a good policy for a couple to travel with the van to ensure that it was positioned most suitably in a siding for our needs at our new destination. This was a practice that was not really approved of, but with train crews usually turning a blind eye, it was actually a very practical option, to avoid error.

"I recall one occasion when our van was being moved a short distance from Ottery St. Mary to Broadclyst, when I and one other decided to keep the fire in the stove alight to provide us with warmth.

"Unexpectedly, the train was halted for a STOP and EXAMINE, and the need for this only became clear when it was realized that smoke from our chimney had alerted a signalman to the possibility of a fire within the train. This led to a PLEASE EXPLAIN procedure, but fortunately without any dire consequences.

"These early months as a railway man were very educational, and I soon began to appreciate the expression, "If you have never drunk tea from a galvanized bucket, with a matchstick floating in it, you will never become a good railway man," something that later engineering students never experienced in their training.

"As I mentioned earlier, my innocent temerity at the Exeter Central depot had earned me a very quick promotion to Assistant Installer. It is also interesting to note that the necessary inherent training for Assistant Lineman, actually took me to the Signalling School at Clapham Junction. (I remember seeing a photograph of the extensive layout used for training in a previous issue of SOUTHERN WAY) and can tell you that this was not only used to train potential signalmen, but also potential Signalling Maintenance Staff.

"I also remember causing amusement among my fellow trainees, and serious consternation for our instructor by playing the following trick on him. We were being shown the intricacies of the single line staff instruments. Repeatedly we were being impressed upon the impossibility of retrieving more than the one staff from the interconnected pair at either end of a single line. As the training instruments were not locked, I surreptitiously inserted my hand into the mechanism of the instrument nearest to me, and manipulated the palls, such that I removed two staffs from my end. I had realized that by removing two the system was replaced into balance.

"The instructor again repeated his emphasis on the impossibility to take out a second staff from either the initial end, or from the opposite end of the single line section, when I horrified him by holding up just one of the two I had surreptitiously removed. His total consternation had to be seen to be appreciated, and he was furious with me for apparently proving that the system was not in fact, totally infallible.

"Having calmed down, he then appreciated that I had actually prematurely demonstrated the approved method of removing the excess number of staffs accumulated at one end, greater than at the other, due to an excess of traffic in one direction, greater than any return traffic. Obviously there was a very strict code of practice in place to allow this action to take place legally, such that an excess even number could be transported back to where the numbers were